Misty

Misty's Long Ride

Across America on Horseback

By

Smooth Georgia Mist

1663 LIBERTY DRIVE, SUITE 200
BLOOMINGTON, INDIANA 47403
(800) 839-8640
WWW.AUTHORHOUSE.COM

First published by AuthorHouse 10/24/05

ISBN: 1-4208-5766-5 (sc)

Printed in the United States of America
Bloomington, Indiana

This book is printed on acid-free paper.

TABLE OF CONTENTS

FOREWARD

In the spring of 1994, I emerged from my mother's womb and into the hands of Lou & Joyce Smith in Argyle, Texas. I had the good fortune to have such a kind couple raise me from a filly to adulthood. I received the best food, medicine, grooming and loving care. They allowed me to be a horse as I frolicked with three other horses on their small ranch. Life was one carefree day after another, season after season. Such was my life for five years.

One day, a tall, lanky stranger visited the ranch. Joyce guided me into a round pen, where she made me walk, trot and lope. The mysterious stranger observed me as I trotted round and around. The next weekend he returned with a truck and trailer. Joyce was leading me, when she broke into tears and threw her arms around my neck. She explained to me this stranger, Howard, would be my new owner and I was leaving her ranch forever. She promised that he would take good care of me and I would have other horses to play with at his ranch. After I hopped into the trailer, I looked back at my mom and two other equine friends. I whinnied long and hard that I did not want to leave but Howard shut the door. Such is the life of a horse.

The next weekend Howard put me in a trailer with my new horse friends, Leah and Scout. After a 30-minute ride, I backed out of the trailer and onto the grounds of the Will Rogers Center in Fort Worth. The next two days Howard led me around the grounds, past hundreds of horses, thousands of cowboys and cowgirls and many new sights and smells. This was my first taste of exploring the world, seeing and feeling something new. Little did I know I had taken my first baby step in preparation for a journey across a continent.

The next weekend Howard guided me around and around in a pen. After a few minutes, he put a saddle pad on me. Then he eased a saddle onto my back for the first time. Since Joyce had assured me that Howard was okay, I trusted what he was doing. A few days later, I felt the pressure of a foot in the left stirrup and then in a slow motion, Howard swung his right leg over the saddle and he was on top of me. It was a shock to have him there but not unpleasant. Soon he had me learning when to go, when to trot and when to stop—on his command.

My education increased in the next few months. Howard trailered me to a lake near Fort Worth where we rode on trails between the trees. I learned what was a threat or danger and what was not. I continued to gain confidence in Howard as a rider and provider.

A year before our Long Ride began, Howard rode me out to US 377 and we spent the morning at a busy intersection. The next week we rode along a seven-lane highway about 10 miles to a coffee shop in Southlake. After a 30-minute stop being tied to a post, we rode home. Screeching tires, police sirens, jack hammers, thundering motorcycles and big 18-wheelers became as common to my senses as squirrels, rabbits and other forest creatures were on nature trail rides. I didn't really know what to think of all this. I met many horses on nature trail rides but Howard and I seemed to be the only ones who navigated urban trail rides.

In the winter of 2002, Howard and I went for a couple of rides along the busy highway at night. That was different! We horses have excellent night vision but the cars now had their headlights on--white on the front and red to the rear. It was just more stuff to become used to and I did.

One morning Howard brought two big boxes to the barn. Out of one, he pulled a brand new saddle that looked like half the size of my normal one. Out of the other, he pulled out various brown bags that he eventually put on top of the new saddle. Innocent of all the items, I accepted what he did. My education and training were coming to a close by March. I was about to embark on a journey that few horses could imagine in the 21st century—coast-to-coast across America.

A couple days later Howard led me into a large, six-horse trailer driven by a stranger. Before leaving me, he promised I would be well cared for until I saw him in two days. Thus began an odyssey that was a life-changing event. I would never be the same again. For the rest of my life, I will never again take for granted steady feed, a comfortable stall and the company of other equines. This is the story of my Long Ride.

Smooth Georgia Mist
Keller, Texas

A MOMENT TO REMEMBER ON THE LONG RIDE

As we rode into Cape Girardeau, Missouri, the sun shined across the waving tree tops on a blustery day. Clouds skidded across the sky. Howard stripped off my saddle at the city limits. I grazed for an hour while Howard ate a candy bar. After a quick stop at the Burger Barn, we moved westward. I smelled the Mississippi River as Howard stopped to let some kids pet me. After a man took some pictures, Howard dismounted and checked all the tie-downs, my cinch, my hooves and my bridle. We must be close to the bridge he had mentioned this morning. Howard seemed nervous and excited. He mounted up, stroked my neck and told me what a magnificent horse I was in all respects.

"Okay Misty girl," he said. "We're going to take a high sidewalk in the sky. No problem for you girl."

He said that today we would complete 1000 miles after we crossed the bridge. We were about to become Long Riders.

Howard halted and waited for a semi-truck to pass. He urged me into a slow trot as I stepped onto the bridge. Immediately I knew we were 200 feet off the ground. My one eye saw through the old, rusting, gray steel girders to an angry river. The wind formed white caps as it tried to push the water back up stream. The crosswind blew 40 miles per hour from the south. As the traffic built up behind us, I felt Howard's tension in his seat and legs. He had good reason.

As my gut tightened, we began crossing the 20 foot wide, rickety two-lane bridge built 80 years ago. When the asphalt ended, there was a steel girder about three feet high and then nothing but air and the river far below. As I moved my head to the right to compensate for no eye, I was none too happy to spot holes where the asphalt met the girder. They were big enough to put my hoof through. I knew if Howard did not help me avoid those holes we would fall over and tumble into the river. I thought he had taken leave of his senses. Why had he not hired a trailer to take me across? Despite Howard giving me good leg cues to stay in the middle of our lane, sometimes the wind blew harder for a bit and we stepped way too near those holes on the edge. Several times he over-compensated and pushed me too far to the left. The on-coming traffic scared me. After a couple of minutes my nerves jangled inside my head. I stopped, pooped and didn't quite know what to do. Where was Texas? My comfortable stall? Would I ever see my buddies back at the corral? What was a horse supposed to do when her owner got a hair-brained idea to ride coast to coast across America?

CHAPTER 1—ALL ABOUT RESPECT IN GEORGIA

Savannah, Georgia—Atlantic Ocean

Sniff, sniff. I smelled the water but something was in it. Salt? Was there such a thing, saltwater? There it was again and this time I was sure of it. Saltwater! I had never smelled it before, but I knew what it was. After 23 hours in the trailer, I was weary and in bad humor. I don't like trailer rides. I usually neither eat nor drink, and sleep was impossible. I only knew I was going to a place called Georgia. My rider Howard had told me that as he walked me into a six-horse trailer. Georgia meant nothing to me. Texas was the only home I knew. I was tired of the trailer and wanted to stretch my legs!

The land flattened out like a pancake a few minutes before we stopped. Dark clouds gathered in the early morning light. The salty smell became more powerful. Finally, the trailer stopped and the diesel engine ceased its throaty exhaust. As the back doors opened, fresh air filled the trailer.

Howard's special whistle "perrss, perrss" broke the quiet of the morning and then his voice boomed into the trailer, "Misty, Misty. How are you girl? How was your ride from Texas?"

I swung my head and saw his tall, lanky frame silhouetted in the doorway. His cowboy hat obscured part of his face except for the moustache. He wore his spurs so I knew we would be riding this day. He clicked the lead rope onto my halter and let me back out of the trailer. If I had known what he had planned for me, I am not sure I would have left the trailer.

"Misty. How are you girl?" a friendly, well-known voice asked me.

I turned my head and saw Joyce, my first owner, approaching. I loved seeing her on this crazy morning.

"You look good Misty and very fit," Joyce said. "Well, you need to be in shape for what you have to do."

She spoke softly with a note of sadness in her voice. Her comments bothered me because; exactly what did I have to do?

"Let me see your right side girl," Joyce requested.

She gasped as she saw the hollow, dark socket where my eye used to be.

"You poor baby," she lamented. "I am so sorry that this has happened."

I had lost the eye several years ago, when Leah kicked me and it became diseased. The pain kept me in agony for three weeks at the vet clinic where they tried all kinds of medicines. I remember Howard crying, when he drove me to the surgeon to remove it. On the surgeon's advice, Howard let the socket become hollow. Being blind on the right side became part of who I was.

While Joyce was talking, Howard had begun to brush me and clean my hooves. The brush felt great as he touched every part of my brown and white coat. He seemed very excited and in a hurry. He threw the new blanket over my back, followed by the new, western saddle. At 22 pounds, it weighed only half of the old one.

Uhgggg! The cantle bag Howard just put on must weigh 20 pounds. The two saddlebags he snapped on weighed another 20 pounds. The final insult was the two small horn bags. Whatever he had in those bags, the total weight exceeded 40 pounds, plus his 195 pounds were going to make for a hard day of riding. He slipped the hackamore bridle (bitless) over my head and mounted up.

We walked in the direction of the white sand, when, what the heck? This was the biggest lake I had ever seen and we headed straight for it. It had waves that broke several feet high. Far out on the lake were two ships as big as 500 trucks each. The beach was a 100 yards wide and in a blink we neared the waves.

Joyce and some others had followed us out to the beach. Howard tried to get me to go into the waves. The waves scared me and after the trailer ride and all this mystery, there was no way was I going into this lake. After a few moments, Howard gave up, dismounted and we walked into the surf.

After we retreated from the waves, Howard put his arms around my neck and began to whisper in my ear.

"Misty, this not a lake you're looking at," Howard said. "It is the Atlantic Ocean and we are headed west to the Pacific Ocean in Oregon. The journey is 3,100 miles long and is going to take six months. We've got hard miles ahead, days without good food or water, and rough living. You and I will often be sleeping in crazy places, mostly without shelter. This will be the hardest thing you and I will ever do. I don't know what I am doing but I promise to do my best to take care of you. I know you can do it, Misty. You have the heart and the head."

My brain exploded in thought, fear and questions. I was stunned. Six months on the road? Nobody rides from coast-to-coast. My mind reeled at the thought of so far to go--these heavy bags and so long without the comforts of home. What about my food, water and shelter from storms? Were we going to ride every day without a break? I did not want to believe what Howard just said but I knew he was serious. It was not a joke. But what is a horse to do? Despite my doubts and fears, Howard turned me and led me back to the parking lot. Thus, the odyssey began.

The skies grew darker and more threatening as Howard put on his rain gear in the parking lot.

"Howard, there is a tornado watch for the next three hours. Shouldn't you and Misty wait till tomorrow to start?" Joyce asked.

"Honestly Joyce, I don't want to start today but we have to reach Oregon before snow closes the passes this fall," Howard said. "We can't stop riding because of wind and rain. We would lose too many days."

'Oh great', I thought. We are starting out in a howling storm. This crazy city slicker is going to be my death or at least a whole lot of discomfort.

As Joyce took our pictures, Howard put his left boot in the stirrup and lifted himself over and into the saddle. The full weight of 264 pounds of Howard, saddle and bags depressed me mentally. I weighed 1050 and this was simply too much for such a long distance. However, Howard did not know this.

As we trotted off on US 82 passing the Tybee Island Motel, the first drops fell from the heavens. As we rounded the corner and headed west, the storm slammed into us with 30 mile per hour winds and sheets of rain. The wind and water swept in from the southwest with unrelenting force. Big trees waved in the tempest's fury. The drops of rain struck like daggers and drove into my eye. Thunder and lightning echoed in my ears. Howard pushed me hard at a fast trot.

My new life dispirited me. Suddenly, "CREATURE–DANGER" flashed into my brain as I leaped sideways into the westbound lane of US 80. The flying creature I quickly realized was a big bird that had flown out of a bush.

Uggghh! Howard's spur dug deeply into my left flank making me veer back onto the shoulder. He was lucky to stay in the saddle, so violent and sudden was my sideways movement. As the large bird climbed higher in the sky, probably more scared than I was,

Howard dismounted. Even through the rain, I could tell he was white with fright.

"Oh my gosh Misty," he said. "If there had been a car coming, we would be dead."

We trotted 18 miles in the next three hours. Even though I was in good condition, the 44 pounds of pack weighed heavy on my back. Worse, the rain had soaked the saddlebags and added even more weight. Luckily, the shoulders remained solid and I was not sinking into mud with each stride.

As we approached the third tall bridge of the morning, the rain began to let up and the wind became pleasant. At the end of the bridge, I saw a sign, which read: "WELCOME TO SAVANNAH, GEORGIA."

No sooner had we entered the city, than a police officer turned on his blue and red overhead lights. Howard and I pulled over.

"Morning officer," Howard said. "Were we speeding?"

The officer cracked a grin before replying that he was concerned for our safety. "What are you doing?" he asked Howard.

"We are riding across America," he replied. "Where you from?" he questioned.

"Texas," Howard said.

Howard rode me relentlessly that first day. I spent most of the afternoon on sidewalks. Combined with unmerciful noise and movements in a city, the day exhausted me. I started dragging my left rear hoof and I knew I was taking off a chunk of the hoof wall.

Two hours before sunset after some 31 miles, Howard directed me into the huge backyard of a church. He ripped off the gear and saddle and put on a lightweight halter for the picket line. Joyce arrived with a bunch of oats. I was so hungry I could eat a bale of hay before you could milk a cow! The day had grown warm, muggy and I sweated profusely after being soaked by the rain.

Joyce led me around the yard to find some of the sparse, spring grass. Howard found a hose for a shower. The water felt good as it began to rinse the salt, sweat and dirt out of my coat. Howard's strong hands massaged my aching muscles as the water cascaded off my back and flanks. I felt almost equine again! Joyce gave Howard food and drink. He pitched his tent while chewing on a sandwich.

As darkness fell, Joyce left and we stood in that church backyard alone. I relaxed and contemplated the day's events. Howard cannot drive me at this pace everyday for six months! Although Howard had worked me into superb condition, we must slow down.

Howard only walked maybe three of the 31 miles, which wasn't much. The arduous day had nearly broken my spirit. Despite the bath and oats, despair filled my heart. I feared this trip was a ship headed for the rocks.

Howard's snoring cut through the night air. I contemplated my life--tied to this picket line thousands of miles from my home in Texas. Finally, late in the night I fell asleep on my feet.

The next morning dawned sunny and warm. Howard broke camp while I enjoyed some oats that

Joyce had left. I was tired and hoped Howard was too.

"Misty, yesterday was a hard day which I hope not to repeat," Howard said. "I am going to try to average about 25 miles a day. We will slow down."

Sure enough, after only about four hours and 14 miles of walking and trotting, we pulled off the main, two-lane road and onto a small ranch. I learned that Joyce had met George and his wife who had invited us to their ranch. Howard stripped off my gear, showered me and put me in a stall with lots of hay and water. This type of stop became quite common in Georgia and Tennessee. Seems like people with horses would take us in two or three nights a week. Works for me! That evening Howard climbed into a horse trailer to sleep while I took advantage of the stall. I lay down in the security of the stall and slept, well, like a horse.

As we were leaving, George told Howard about the 8-foot alligator, which he had killed last week in the pond in front of his house. Oh great! Something else for me to worry about! I had never seen an alligator but it did not sound friendly.

Rested and well fed, I felt great and took off at a fast trot. After an hour or so Howard started to walk a bit more. We stopped at a store along US 80. Howard returned shortly with a tube of ointment. After we trotted out of town, he stopped and put some of the cream on his butt. He told me he had two good-sized saddle sores from the day of rain and hard riding. So he too had suffered on the rough first day! After a couple of hours we pulled into a long driveway. A couple of other horses ran up to the fence and nickered at me.

"Hey guys," I nickered back. "How is the food and hay here? I'm starved!"

I wanted to say more but Howard directed me to the barn. Howard gave me a lunch of oats and it was nice to stop a little early.

The owners, Bill and Melanie, showed up later and we all got acquainted. Melanie was checking out her horse in the breezeway, when I saw her stalled stallion pin his ears back. Ohh oh! He is going to bite her. A moment later the stallion indeed reached out and bit her on the shoulder before she could react. She let out a scream and Howard rushed over to help her. The teeth had ripped through her shirt but there was only a little blood.

"That's it!" Melanie screamed. "I am having you gelded on Monday!"

I am not sure what being gelded meant but it didn't sound like fun. I know a couple of stallions in my corral back in Texas had been gelded. They moped around for six months feeling sorry for themselves. Never could figure that out, but then again, I'm a female.

Howard disappeared after feeding me dinner and I savored the security and warmth of the stall.

The flat-as-a-pancake land changed the next day into a carpet with small wrinkles. We trotted along a tunnel of tall trees. The warm, mild weather made for another good traveling day. Still, the weight of the pack made it hard going and Howard was only walking about 10 percent of the distance. I am not getting enough grass or feed, even when we stop at a barn for the night. How do I tell Howard what I need?

After another night in a barn we rode 30 miles and stopped at twilight. Howard found another barn for me while he pitched his tent in the back yard. A 20 mile per hour wind beat against me all the next day. Our luck with ranchers ran out. Near dark, Howard directed me into a forest of pine trees.

He took 10 minutes preparing my picket line between two trees, ripping down limbs and anything else that might hurt me. I drank water at the last town but I received no dinner. I was hungry after such a long day. It drizzled as Howard crawled into his tent.

I fell fast asleep, but then heard a twig snap. I pulled back on my lead rope, trying to move away from the sound. I couldn't see what made the noise and I didn't know if it was a lion or one of those alligators. I whirled to the left, then the right and backwards trying to get loose and run away! In my efforts I realized that I had stepped over the picket line and it was wrapped around my front leg. I couldn't move! I would be killed and eaten--bound up there unable to flee.

Howard emerged from his tent naked as a jaybird. I didn't quite know what to do with that! He called to me, trying to calm me down. The flashlight was in his teeth as he asked me to stand still and lift up my front leg, which was held fast by the rope.

My eye was still glued to the dark, ominous forest--which made so many sounds. My thrashing and spinning could easily mean my hoof would come down on his bare foot, breaking it. I had to trust Howard to untangle me, so I stopped thrashing and lifted my leg. A few moments later, I was free. Howard stayed with me for a few minutes to signal that he would take care of me no matter what. It would not be the last time Howard would have to untangle me from my picket line.

I gained some confidence that he would watch over and help me.

The drizzle continued till dawn as Howard broke camp and tacked me up. The temperature had dropped to near freezing. We were clearing the forest when the rain and wind struck from the rear. Raindrops lashed my butt--instantly soaking me. This storm was worse than the first day and lasted for two hours. Like magic, it stopped. The clouds broke and the sun shone on us for the first time in two days.

Howard shivered as he stopped at a diner. He tied me to a grassy area nearby, allowing me to graze on lush grass. A traveler came up and offered me an apple but I spit it out. I don't like them. I wished she had brought carrots. I love carrots.

The rain had made the shoulder so soft my hooves sank in two inches with every step. It doubled the energy I needed to go the same distance. Howard walked 10 percent of the time. By the time Howard stopped at a ranch, I was exhausted.

"Here you go girl," he said. "I found you some oats and hay."

The cold, wet start to the day seemed to have zapped a lot of his energy, too. That evening he talked to two other guys while I munched on grass under the picket line.

We headed out after sunrise and a few minutes later entered the town of Dublin, Georgia. We stopped at the local feed store. Howard found some oats and I munched ravenously. Hunger stalked me all the time. While Howard watched me eat, a woman from the store came out.

She turned to Howard.

"I have always wanted to marry a real cowboy," she said. "Are you available?"

I looked up from my feed and I think I saw Howard turn a little red as he replied, "That depends ma'am. Right now, I've got to cross this continent on horseback."

We left with Howard leading me through the town. Thank you, Howard. The concrete sidewalks are tough on my joints, especially with his weight upon me.

Outside of Dublin we turned north on US 441. So far the shoulders had been wide and fairly level. Pine trees lined the highway. Howard often moved me a little to the left or right to avoid all the obstacles: beer and whiskey bottles, 2 X 4s with nails, thrown tire tread and other assorted debris that might hurt me. Although he wore spurs, he never used them except to help me miss dangerous objects. We were trotting along when a van pulled up going the other way and stopped.

The driver called out to Howard, "Hey, do you need any food?"

"No," Howard replied.

"How about your horse's hooves? They okay? I am a farrier."

Howard let out a little scream.

"Eeooow," he said. "Yes, she needs a new left rear."

The man pulled around behind us and stopped. He introduced himself as Tommie Wilson. Howard took off the packs and saddle.

"I'd say you are about due for four new shoes," he told Howard. "I'll just go ahead and do them all." In the next 45 minutes he stripped off my old shoes and nailed on four new ones.

"What do I owe you?" Howard asked.

"Your thanks is enough," he replied.

Howard protested but in the end no money changed hands.

Days and miles wore on. The weight of the packs bore down on my back and withers. My hair thinned out where the cantle and saddlebags rested on my rump and sides. I dropped weight every day yet Howard still did not seem to be able to reverse the problem. We had been traveling only a week but it seemed like forever. When Howard didn't find a barn for me, he hooked me up to my picket line in some forest. I suffered little sleep--as I remained awake looking for lions and alligators. Especially those alligators! Whatever they are, even the name sounds scary!

The constant 25-27 mile days wore on me. Ten days out I finally enjoyed a break. After we left Milledgeville, Georgia, we turned off US 441 and onto a side street. After tying me up to a tree, Howard turned and gave me some great news.

"Misty, we are going to stay here for a day off," he said. "The rest of today and all tomorrow will be rest time. I will try to get you a day off every week."

With those words, Howard led me to a grassy five-acre paddock, took off my bridle and I was free. I dropped down and rolled to get that itch off my back. When I stood up, I noticed two other horses coming up to say "Hi."

We got acquainted after which I dropped down in the grass and enjoyed the warm sunshine pouring through a few white clouds. With my equine buddies watching over me, I drifted off into deep sleep.

Later that evening Howard stopped by to give me a scoop of oats, which I horsed down in a hurry. I was still hungry and wished I could tell him it was okay to give me more. He looked me over.

"Misty, I can see you are losing weight and I'd like to give you more grain," he said. "However, the vet said never to give you more than one scoop of grain because you might colic. I am sorry. Maybe you can gain some weight back tomorrow."

"Oh, Howard", I wanted to say, "I can't gain back 40 pounds in one day by eating spring grass. I appreciate your concern but you are clueless."

The day off was nice but all too brief. It rained pretty hard in the morning and only stopped just before we left. At least Howard looked a little better and smelled a lot better. I know he was going days without a shower and his clothes got dirty in a hurry. He must have been able to solve those issues during our day off.

A few nights later the temperature fell to well below freezing. Since I had already lost my winter hair coat, I shivered. Howard had not packed my blanket. Thank goodness this trip rarely left me this cold. We camped out behind a ranger station near Madison. Howard awoke twice during the night to untangle my lead rope. At dawn, Howard emerged from his tent.

"Okay Misty, I am going to let you graze while I break camp," he said. "I am putting the hobbles on your front legs. You have had them on before, so no big deal."

Howard led me to a grassy area, attached the hobbles and went back to the tent. I was munching the tasty grass, when I heard and saw something in the underbrush of the forest. I launched myself in the opposite direction. Even in hobbles I moved pretty fast, leaping like a kangaroo. I hopped 30 yards to the edge of the meadow, where I decided to stop and see if the creature was still after me.

"Misty," Howard cried in a low voice. "Easy girl, steady, no problem here, please don't run."

Howard's eyes grew wide with fear and amazement. I guess he didn't know if I would hop all the way back to Texas! I let him come up to me and stroke my neck as he called out to me. After a few minutes he took off the hobbles and let me graze. He now realized that I could run with or without them.

As Howard led me by the ranger station, I spotted something dead in the brush. He saw it too and stopped.

"It's a bobcat Misty," Howard said. "Even dead it's a thing of beauty. Probably killed by a car or truck. Let's take that as a lesson."

The cold morning air lingered for hours as we trotted northward. After about two hours Howard stopped at a restaurant. Howard shivered as he tied me to a light pole in the grass. His hands shook and he had trouble making his fingers move. The sun broke out behind the clouds and felt good on my now bare back. Between mouthfuls of grass, I noticed Howard drinking coffee non-stop for a half-hour.

Early in the afternoon, I stepped in a small hole and Howard reined me to a halt.

"You okay girl?" he inquired.

The jolt had not felt good but I thought I was okay. Howard led me for the next half mile, and then we ran together for a few yards. He inspected my neck to see if I would have the characteristic bobbing motion, which would indicate I was lame. My neck was rock steady, indicating no problem. He remounted and we rode through the southern end of Athens, Georgia.

At the edge of town with darkness descending, Howard put up a picket line in the trees next to a large church. Without any warning, I felt a plastic tube in my mouth squirting some gook that tasted horrible!

"Sorry girl," Howard said. "I had to give you some Bute, in case you hurt yourself today."

'Okay', I thought, Bute was like aspirin and would be good for any minor injury. It tasted so bad!

After pitching his tent, Howard led me around back and let me graze for an hour in the light of the street lamps. After hooking me, he disappeared into the church for a few minutes. A short time later, I noticed a lot of people leaving the church. About 15 minutes later one of the cars drove back into the parking lot. A woman got out of her car and headed our way.

"Hello, Mr. Cowboy," she said. "Are you awake?"

Howard's voice returned from his tent, "Yes ma'am, I'm awake. What's going on?"

"Here is a blanket I can loan you for the night," she said. "Just leave it in the church office tomorrow morning. "

"Thank you so much." he replied. "I was going to freeze tonight, even with my horse blanket over my sleeping bag."

The woman departed and moments later Howard's snoring broke the silence of the cold, windless night. He sounded like a slow moving locomotive all night long.

I felt fine as we left the church at sunrise. As the day progressed however, my front left ankle began aching as the Bute wore off. After our lunch stop I started bobbing my head to take the weight off the ankle. Howard noticed that pretty quickly and dismounted.

"Oh girl," he exclaimed. "You did hurt yourself yesterday. Dang it anyway!"

He made me take more Bute, before he led me through the town of Jeffersonville. We walked to a ranch with horses just north of town. No one was home and Howard let me graze on the sparse grass of the yard for several hours. At dark he hooked me to a picket line under an equipment shed, next to which, he pitched his tent. I smelled rain in the air and possibly a storm, so I enjoyed being in a shelter for the night. Howard sat down on a bench to enjoy his meal of bread, honey and peanut butter. He called somebody on his cell phone, describing my lameness.

"Good news girl," he said. "Lou and Joyce will be here tomorrow to pick us up and go back to their farm. You'll see the vet and then rest as long as you need to get better."

Two hours after dark Howard walked away, returning after a few minutes. Howard took down his tent.   What are you doing?

"Sorry Misty girl," he said. "The caretakers of the ranch have ordered us to leave. The fact that you are lame and it is going to storm meant nothing to them. I am sorry. It is going to be a miserable night."

Minutes later he led me down the driveway. We walked about two miles next to the highway before stopping. Howard had his strobe light out, which signaled the drivers that we were on the side of the road. Howard and I had practiced some night traveling, so the headlights were no big deal. I was perplexed and disturbed as to how those equine owners could be so mean to me.

Howard led me into some trees above a small restaurant. As he cleared the area where the picket line was, it began raining. By the time he crawled into his tent it was pouring while lightning flashed all around us. This small forest was not to my liking as I thrashed around all night, not sleeping a wink.

The miserable night gave way to a drizzly, soggy dawn. Howard exited his tent muttering to himself. I shivered from cold rain and the temperature, hovering in the mid 40s. Howard saddled me up, walked me down to the restaurant and tied me to a pole in the grass. He removed everything but the saddle and walked inside. The saddle did keep the cold rain off my back.

Two hours later Lou and Joyce drove up with a horse trailer and I happily climbed in. We drove for an hour, arriving at the vet clinic near Epworth, GA. The lady vet put me through a couple of tests.

"She does not have a major problem," she said to Howard. "That is the good news. Give her two grams of Bute twice a day for the next four days. I'll check her again on Sunday."

I saw Howard smile broadly at this good news. I knew it was not a big problem. A few minutes later we pulled into the ranch of Lou and Joyce.

"Mom? Is that you?" I whinnied.

I could hardly believe my eye. Howard released me into the four-acre pasture where my mom ran up to greet me. We rubbed noses. It had been two years since Howard had put me in his trailer and turned my life upside down. I told her about this 'long ride' that I was taking Howard on. She was appalled but interested. We spent a wonderful afternoon in the warm sun of a Georgia spring.

The next three days spelled heaven. I munched grass all day long and slept securely in a stall next to my mom at night. The only bad thing was the Bute twice a day but Howard always gave some grain after each dose as a reward. My ankle felt fine after two days and I stopped limping. I enjoyed being with my mom again and we swapped a lot of stories. She had been on many trail rides with Joyce but nothing as crazy as what I was doing. She could not imagine riding next to a busy US highway with cars and trucks nearby only a few feet off her rump. I proudly explained it was no big deal once you get used to it. I told her Howard and I had gone for many urban trail rides back in Fort Worth, Texas, gaining experience to be safe during this ride across America.

On the fourth day a lot of people started showing up at noon. Lou and Joyce threw a party and many people wanted to get a look at the horse and rider who thought they could ride across America. The vet arrived, checked me out and pronounced me good to go. A cheer arose from the crowd when she made the announcement.

'Uh oh', I thought.

That meant my four days in heaven ended and it was back on the road. That news sure took the party spirit out of me. Yeah, like, let's go plow the back forty acres for a fun horse day!

The next morning Howard led me into the trailer. After an hour or so on a curvy highway, I saw the restaurant where we had camped out. At least it was a nice spring day--not too hot, not too cold. Howard walked me a quarter mile to loosen up, then he climbed into the saddle. He continued the practice of having me trot 60 percent of the time, walk 30 percent and he would lead me about 10 percent of the distance. Even with the four days at the ranch I was still nearly 100 pounds underweight. Losing the weight caused my saddle to fit improperly and I had two points on the withers where I was losing hair. I was also losing hair on my flanks because the cinch came too close to the D ring on the saddle. I believe Howard knew there was a problem because he fussed with those four areas for a few days. Still, not much had really changed.

In the late afternoon Howard directed me up another church driveway. In the back were many little boys and girls playing soccer. A whole bunch of them came running over as Howard jumped off. I am used to all the attention and enjoyed the little hands petting me on the shoulder and sides. Howard stayed busy keeping their little feet from getting too close to my hooves. If something ever spooked me and I moved quickly, I might break all their little toes.

Howard stripped my packs and let me munch as the games continued. I ate for two hours before Howard tied me up to the picket line. This night the rope was strung up between the ends of a goal post. Howard threw up his tent behind the net. He fed me some oats he had put in the saddlebags, plus I had all the fresh water I could drink. Since I could see a long ways across the fields, I slept pretty well that night.

Before dawn the next day clouds skidded across the starry sky. Moments later I saw the first flashes of lightning and soon after felt the first raindrops. Howard popped out his tent and began to break camp in a hurry. Much to my delight he gave me some oats. It was raining and thundering pretty good by the time he had me loaded up and we left the soccer field. Howard led me just a few yards down the highway, stopping at a café. He took off the saddlebags but left everything else on me. He tied my rein to a wooden post, which held up some banner and went inside. The lightning was a bit scary and the crack of thunder was close.

"CRACK, BOOM!" screamed into my ears.

I jerked my head violently to the right, causing the wooden post to come out of the ground. I began to run in total panic with the wooden post and the banner beside me, banging into my legs.

I ran across the first two lanes of westbound traffic, bounded through the median in two strides and crossed the eastbound lanes as more thunder and lightning struck nearby. The thick, rush-hour traffic slammed on its brakes, missing me by only a few feet.

"Misty!" I heard Howard scream as he emerged from the restaurant. I just kept running up the hill, dragging the 4x4 and banner. I was getting out of that area no matter what! I crested the hill, galloped a few more yards and then saw some quality grass. I slammed on the brakes, took a breath, looked around and started munching.

Moments later Howard came over the ridge, blowing great clouds of steam from his mouth, obviously out of breath. He stopped running and started talking to me.

"Easy Misty girl," he said. "You're okay. You really know how to scare a guy."

I kept eating while he rubbed his hands over parts of my body, probably looking for injuries. He untied my reins from the 4x4 and dragged the post away from me. The loud thunder and close lightning strikes were no longer present as the storm moved southward. A small truck drove up and the manager of the gas station put the 4x4 and the banner in the bed.

"I am really sorry about the damage my horse caused," Howard told the man. "How much do I owe you?"

The manager saw the 4x4 was undamaged, the banner was okay and the only damage was the broken rope.

"Don't worry about it," he said. "No real problem here. It sure was exciting to watch her run across the street and miss all the cars. This will be a great story to tell my customers and friends."

Howard led me back to the store. This time he tied me up to something near the gas pumps. He went inside for just a moment, returning with a plate of food and his coffee.

"Oh Misty," he said. "I am so glad you're okay. What am I going to do with you? You could have been killed by a car! You just used up one of your lives today."

He sat down on the concrete and finished his breakfast, eyeing me nervously every few moments.

Finally finished, Howard mounted up and we rode off into the steady rain. Hour after hour we rode in that miserable cool rain. We never stopped until late afternoon. Howard parked me under the overhang of a restaurant, stripped off all my gear and walked inside to eat. He ate his late lunch in a booth next to where I stood outside. I was so tired I could hardly stand up. The muddy footing made me work twice as hard to cover the miles.

After about 20 minutes, Howard came out just as a man arrived and started taking my picture. As Howard talked, the man wrote down stuff on his pad. After the man left, Howard saddled me back up. We rode only for a few minutes before stopping in the middle of a small town.

Moments later a truck with horse trailer arrived and in I hopped. We drove about 10 minutes out of town before stopping at a mobile home. Howard's new friend had a small barn where they put me. I got a scoop of grain and all the hay I could eat.

"Howard," I wanted to scream, "I need more oats than this. I am losing more weight and the four spots that have bothered me are getting worse. Help!"

Of course, I couldn't talk to him and I just had to do the best I could. We continued traveling an average of 25 miles a day and no relief in sight.

Howard's new friend trailered us back to the middle of that town the next morning. Howard tied me outside a restaurant, went inside and returned with his plate of food and coffee. After yesterday's events, I guess he was taking no chances.

It was a long day of trotting and walking. The heavy bags on my rump area strained my knees and ankles. They wore me down. Also, the hair on my point of the hip was wearing thin over a large area as the friction took its toll. I was becoming a real mess.

To my surprise, I ended that 31-mile day by hopping into Lou and Joyce's horse trailer. We took a short ride back to their ranch where I spent the night in a stall. The next day was warm and sunny and a day off without being ridden. That helped a little but I was a train about to jump the tracks.

The next morning they trailered us back to the spot we were picked up.

"Okay girl," Howard said. "I dropped a few items at Lou & Joyce's that will lighten your load a bit."

I noticed that the saddlebags weighed a little less but were still very heavy. It was something--but not much.

A few hours later Howard had me get in line at a Dairy Queen. We had done this several times and it always entertained the drivers and the employees. Howard ordered his usual large Blizzard. We parked ourselves in some thick grass in the median. As Howard enjoyed his sweet treat, I munched the tall, lush grass.

The small mountains of north Georgia rose high on the horizon that day. Howard walked up a lot of the hills. He rode me down the hills but that was a mistake. My thin spots in the withers became much worse that day. Riding me downhill, the saddle pushed into my withers with each stride making the two tender spots much worse. Like Howard said on the first day, he just didn't know what he was doing.

We had no luck finding a barn and had to camp in the forest.

A cool, misty drizzle greeted us the next morning. A gray sky spread from horizon to horizon. I hoped it would not become worse and make the bags gain weight. We were plodding along US 76 west of Chatsworth, Georgia when a strange sight appeared through the light fog and mist. Howard stopped me and set me T to the highway. He took off his Stetson and placed it over his heart. As he did, a long line of slow moving cars, all with their headlights on, approached from the west. The first couple of cars were black limousines with little purple flags flapping on their hoods. A chauffeur drove by me with a sullen face. Behind him, another limousine carried a family. The mother dabbed tears from her eyes with a handkerchief while the children sat with eyes staring forward. Silver spray kicked up from the wheel wells of the passing cars. Car after car passed with sad faces staring forward. Howard sat motionless in the saddle. The last vehicle was a pickup truck driven by an old man wearing a cowboy hat. As he passed, I saw the weathered cowboy touch his hand to the brim of his hat toward Howard. Instantly, Howard reached forward with his hat in hand to the old man whose face was filled with sadness. I had seen Howard do that before though I had no idea why.

"That was a funeral Misty," Howard said, solemnly. "Someone died and was about to be put to rest. We always stop when that happens girl. It's all about respect."

The last vehicle vanished in the gray mist. Howard placed his hat back on his head and we continued westward at a walk.

We spent the next couple of days going due west. The month of April became warm and I lathered up under the saddle pad. The synthetic pad was not doing a good job--neither with the friction nor wicking away the sweat. East of Tunnel Hill something dropped out of Howard's blue backpack and onto my rump. A few minutes later, Howard stopped and yelled. We backtracked a hundred yards as Howard located some of the items. Howard's mood turned very somber and I thought he might cry. Trying to save the hair on my withers, he had put the contents of the two horn bags in his backpack. Somehow the zipper had come loose and now he had lost equipment. The event was another indicator of the problems on the trip thus far.

After spending the night at a highway construction site, we rode through a few miles of open country. Heading straight north for a few miles, I saw a sign ahead of us: "WELCOME TO TENNESSEE." The other read: "CHATTANOOGA CITY LIMITS."

Though we had completed the first state, I knew the sores on my skin were about to bring this trip to a halt.

Howard dismounted and walked me on the city sidewalks.

CHAPTER 2—TENNESSEE WALKING HORSES

Howard walked me for two miles as we passed densely packed houses along St. Elmo Street. After a quick lunch, he mounted up and rode me the next two miles on asphalt. The four-lane road went straight up. Tough climbing! The day grew hot, muggy and the saddlebags heavy. Howard had no choice as there was neither sidewalk nor shoulder. Finally we hit a stretch of businesses and Howard led me for a mile. After a few minutes we left the city and were once again out among the trees and grass.

We trotted by a large river to our right, which I saw through the leafless trees. I maintained a trot though it required a big effort. After two hours I spotted a large bridge up ahead. It was old and gray and looked very narrow. As we approached it, I felt Howard's tension building in his seat. He grew nervous which made me anxious, too. We had never crossed such a tall bridge. The water swirled 100 feet below the bridge and there was no protection to keep us from falling off.

Howard trotted me onto the bridge. The traffic was light, though several cars stacked up behind us. A light wind blew while Howard kept me in the center of our westbound lane. Howard's tension came through loud and clear as we passed the halfway point.

"Easy Misty girl," he said. "No real problem here. You can do it."

I kept my eye on the trees at the end of the bridge and focused on getting off. After three minutes, we reached the other side and I felt the big release of tension on Howard's part. He jumped off and hugged my neck.

"What a horse you are Misty! You're the best."

More hugs and kisses on my neck followed, as he led me the next mile.

It was nice to have him off my back because I was tired and the thin spots had grown larger than a quarter and totally devoid of hair. Hugs and kisses were nice but no substitute for food and less weight on my back.

Howard stopped for his dinner at a restaurant and as usual did not take off the saddle or bags. He did not understand my back needed to breathe and dry out as often as possible.

Right after his dinner Howard made camp in some trees near Jasper on US 41. Finally, he saw the raw flesh on my skin in four spots.

"Oh Misty," he said. "You are a mess and it is all my fault. I am so sorry to cause you this injury and pain. I can't ride you like this."

He broke into tears and cried for several minutes. He had learned that his lack of knowledge had hurt me and derailed the trip. His crying told me he cared, making it less likely he would injure me again. The only question left was whether we could put the train back on the tracks.

The next morning Howard examined my bare spots again. I wondered what he would do different this morning. First he threw the saddle pad on my back, then moved it back about eight inches. Next came the saddle and the baggage. He tightened the cinch in the new spot. All four of my bare spots were exposed to the air and would not suffer any further irritation. However, if Howard mounted up with the saddle so far back, he would be putting pressure on my kidneys, which would hurt me in a number of ways.

I steeled myself for that foot in the stirrup and the pain that would follow.

"Come on girl," Howard said. "I will not cause you any extra grief. I have done enough already. We have been invited to a ranch near here. Let's hope we can spend more than a night there."

Howard grabbed my reins and walked me off the campsite.

Howard led me some eight miles that morning. The route we took led us out along a country road and onto a private drive. At the cattle guard I saw a herd of horses frolicking in a pasture.

Howard met an older couple, spoke for several minutes then led me to a barn 400 yards from the main house. He stripped off all my gear and gave me a long shower with soap and everything. It had been days since I had a shower and it felt heavenly.

The woman had accompanied us to the barn. After my shower she looked closely at my bare spots.

"What do you think, Mrs. Chalupsky?" Howard asked.

"You're right," she replied, "you cannot ride her until those spots are fully covered with hair. Do you know what caused them?"

"I think so," Howard said. "I called the saddle maker last night and described what had happened the past three weeks. He said all four spots were caused by the loss of weight, which caused the saddle to fit improperly. The saddle began pinching her in those four spots and after 500 miles, you see the results."

"Did he have any suggestions besides keeping the weight on?" she asked.

"Yes, he recommended a wool pad should be used in addition to the saddle blanket," Howard said. "He said I should never let the cinch ring get closer than four inches from the saddle D ring. I had the two get within two inches of each other, which caused two of the bare spots.

"Lastly he said to protect the withers, I should ride her up the hills and lead her down, the opposite of what I had done in Georgia," Howard said.

"Sounds like you don't know much about what you're doing," she said.

"I know how to ride and take care of a horse under normal circumstances, but no," Howard said, "I don't have a clue on what I'm doing now. I spoke to dozens of experienced riders and trainers before I left but none had any experience doing what we are doing. Even the endurance riders I spoke to could not help because they always have a trailer every night. Nobody knows anything about what we are doing."

"Sounds like you better find out quickly or you'll never see Oregon," she said. "Misty is going to need a good three weeks to cover those bare spots. If she loses her hair again, you'll never reach Oregon before winter."

Howard put me in one-acre paddock, fed me grain and threw some hay. While I wolfed down the grain, he and Mrs. Chalupsky continued their conversation.

"Mrs. Chalupsky," Howard said. "It is a lot to ask but is there any chance Misty and I can stay here while she heals? I'd be happy to work hard doing whatever you need."

"Call me Mildred," she replied. "Actually you and I are in luck. My hired hand just quit this morning. You can stay in the bunkhouse next to the barn. The judge and I will feed you and Misty in exchange for helping out around the ranch. We have 26 horses and 80 head of cattle so there is always something to do."

Howard shook her hand and thanked her profusely for the offer. I was relieved, too. It meant I would have three weeks off with good food, water and shelter. 'This is good', I thought to myself.

The next three weeks sped by with me in bliss. I enjoyed a stall every night and turned out to the paddock every day. When it rained, Howard put me in the dry stall. Howard rode me everyday. However, he rode me bareback and only for an hour or so. After having him on my back for seven hours per day, that was a slice of carrot.

There was a big and welcome change in my feed after a few days. Howard fed me oats four times a day, instead of just morning and night. He brought alfalfa pellets full of good nutrients. All that plus always having either grass or hay to eat, I gained back all the weight I had lost.

I saw Howard working around the ranch. He mended fences, fed hay to the cattle, cut down dead trees, mucked out the barn and many other chores, working a lot of hours.

Near the end of the three weeks Howard came over one afternoon after chores were done.

"Misty, I have exciting news," he said. "I was contacted by an organization which knows all about what we are doing. It is called The Long Riders Guild. I spoke to the founder, CuChullaine O'Reilly, and he and others have given me dozens of tips on how to make our trip successful. You will see the changes as soon as we leave here in a few days."

All too soon the three weeks of rest and healing came to an end. On a cool, cloudy morning Howard told me we were leaving. The first change was a nice, woolen Indian blanket. 'That wool felt so much better', I thought. Next came a stiff pad also made of wool. Then came the usual lightweight western saddle but it did not have the rear cinch, making it a pound lighter. The cantle bag came on next and it was a little lighter than usual. I waited for the saddlebags and horn bags but they never came! Apparently, you can teach an old cowboy new tricks!

Howard walked me the quarter mile to the main house where Mildred and the Judge waited to say goodbye. Moments later, we trotted off the property and onto the shoulder of a small road. After lugging some 44 pounds across the state of Georgia, just having the 18 pound cantle bag made my day! This new lightweight was going to make my life a lot easier.

Howard urged me into a slow canter which I was happy to do. After so much rest, back at my normal weight and having not been ridden hard in three weeks, I wanted to run! I galloped pretty hard, enjoying the exercise. After two miles Howard reined me to a stop and hopped off. That was different. He led me for a about a mile, hopped back on and loped me for another two miles. As he dismounted to lead me again, I noticed his new footwear. He had changed his cowboy boots and heavy spurs for hiking boots and lightweight spurs. Obviously, he was prepared for some serious walking.

This lope/walk pattern took up the morning, as we approached the biggest mountain I had ever seen.

"Okay Misty," Howard said. "That is Monteagle in front of us and it will be a very tough five mile climb."

Howard directed me onto a small side road called Old Stagecoach Road, which featured a narrow shoulder. We climbed. I walked up the steep shoulder for about a mile, before Howard jumped off to lead me the next mile. We switched off and on until we had reached the summit two hours later. Looking back we saw the sweep of the valley now all green with the new spring leaves.

We returned to the pattern of two miles at an easy lope, followed by Howard leading me for a mile. In this manner we moved along the crest of Monteagle. At the town of Monteagle Howard stopped for lunch. Though we stopped for only 20 minutes, he did something else different. He stripped off everything, which allowed my back to dry off. Thanks Howard! He also fed me five pounds of oats he had brought with him. Before he ate, he filled my two gallon collapsible bucket. When we left Monteagle, I had been well fed, watered, cooled off and felt refreshed.

Though the miles were still tough, Howard's new approach made me a happy horse! We passed over one of those interstate highways as we left the restaurant. On the outskirts of town on US 41 we descended Monteagle. There wasn't much traffic and no trucks. I guess they were on the expressway. Howard led me three of the four miles, which had a steep angle. He was really watching out for my withers. We were taking a break at the bottom of the mountain--when a white pickup truck slowed down and stopped.

"You need a place to stay tonight?" the woman driver called out to Howard.

"Sure do, ma'am," Howard said. "We'd appreciate it."

"My name is Sheila and this is my son Thomas," she said. "We're headed for a meeting and won't be home for about three hours. Here is a garage door opener. Take care of your horse in our barn, then go on in the house and make yourself at home. We just live a mile down the road."

Barn? Did somebody say barn? That lady knows how to make a horse happy. Howard's newfound way of riding had made the day a lot easier but still it had been a hard, 25-mile day. Howard leaned way over the saddle and watched the woman drop the garage door opener in his blue backpack. Howard loped me that mile and in no time we arrived.

Howard gave me a shower before putting me in a stall. He poured grain and added hay into the feeder. He filled up two buckets with water before giving me a kiss and leaving me to munch. This was living after a hard day.

Howard came back out after two hours. He had showered himself and he had a soda in his hand.

"Hey girl," Howard said. "How are you doing? I am pooped after walking 10 miles today. That shower felt great and this soda is good for my soul."

He poured out another scoop of grain into my feeder. I stopped eating the hay and attacked the grain. That evening he came out and poured another scoop of grain.

Next day, we rode out a couple hours after sunrise on a cold, crisp spring day, which showed a hint of mist in the air. As I pounded up the first rolling hill, my nostrils belched steam.

"I am a Knight of the Round Table and Misty is my faithful steed," Howard cried out. "Together we go forth to slay dragons and save the princess."

Forget the dragons and a princess, Howard; I want a barn, stall and a handsome stallion!

After he hopped off for his one-mile walk, Howard said he was kidding and we were not going to slay any dragon. 'Good', I thought. I had no desire to meet a dragon.

After grueling climbs and descents the day before, rolling hills felt easier on my legs. Trees lined the road, which kept the wind at a minimum. Two miles on with one mile off made my day go fast. The cloudy skies gave way to dark clouds in the afternoon. Howard directed me into a business with a lot of cars and it had a few horses in the side yard.

"Good news, Misty," Howard exclaimed. "The owner of the body shop is going to let us stay here tonight."

A few minutes later he led me to a one half-acre turnout with a small shed. I started dinner off with sweet feed and a couple of flakes of hay. Even when the rain pelted the ground, I felt good about the day. I moved into the shelter and lay down. Life was pretty good!

Before daybreak, Howard came out of the office where he had slept to give me two more scoops and two more flakes. We stopped at the west edge of Manchester for Howard to eat breakfast. An hour later I noticed something very strange in the trees. All kinds of stuff hung in the leaves and branches, while several buildings had either lost their roofs or were completely destroyed.

"Wow," Howard shouted. "Check it out Misty! I read a tornado raced through here two weeks ago. Two people died. What a mess!"

Just as I was getting hungry, Howard stopped and led me up a private driveway. After a few words with a woman, Howard tied me and headed toward a barn outback. Moments later he put the blue backpack, now holding grain, on the ground for me to munch. I had been eating for two minutes, when a big pickup drove up. Howard walked over to talk to the driver and started chatting like he always did.

Suddenly the driver yelled at Howard, "Get your horse and get off my land."

"Yes sir, no problem," Howard replied.

He took the feed away and led me down the driveway. Humans! Can't a horse eat in peace? We stopped just a few yards down the highway where Howard let me finish my lunch. Never did figure out what his problem was! Soon we galloped down US 41 again; the loud man became a bad memory.

In the afternoon the good shoulder since Savannah vanished. Clink, clink, clink went my shoes as Howard had to ride me at a trot on the asphalt. Sometimes he was able to lope me for short distances in the ditch but the lack of shoulders made it tough on my body. After eight miles, I smelled horses and I hoped Howard did, too.

Good! Howard jumped off and tied me up to Eddie Howland Stables. Shortly thereafter Howard walked me into a stall followed by a dinner of oats, hay and water. Looking up, I saw a woman bring Howard a plate of steaming chicken, greens and potatoes. He ate ravenously and the food vanished. Later that evening I watched him and a bunch of other people around a bonfire on the north edge of the barn. Before calling it a night, Howard dropped another scoop of grain in the bucket plus more hay.

"Your stomach will be happier from now on Misty girl," Howard explained. "The Long Riders Guild taught me how to feed you lots of food safely. You will receive 20 pounds of grain everyday I can find it for you."

The night grew cold but I was fine in the windless stall. Howard fed me in the pre-dawn light and we departed by sunrise. He said he spent the night in the horse trailer, which helped him stay warm. As we left the small village, the shoulder reappeared and it was nice to lope on the right surface! The sunny cool day was perfect for traveling and we made the most of it.

Late in the afternoon Howard led me through the city of Murfreesboro. On the west edge he led me into a church parking lot. After a few words with a man at the door, he walked me to a baseball field in the back. After he shut all the gates and doors, he turned me loose for the night. Howard disappeared into the church. He came out several times that evening to check on me and re-fill my water bucket. On the last of those checks he let me know about his evening.

"Misty, I hope this lush grass in the baseball field is enough," Howard said. "I was invited to eat with the family who just lost a loved one. I hope I didn't embarrass myself by eating too much. The widow invited me to the memorial service and another woman invited me to a two-hour revival service. It was interesting! I am bedding down in the barn over there on top of some straw."

I felt pretty safe in the baseball field so after hours of munching, I fell asleep.

Before dawn Howard came over and I saw him shivering and his teeth chattered. He tacked me up and led me out of the church parking lot. Like all mornings since leaving the Chalupsky's ranch, he walked me a quarter mile before hopping on. That was a good thing because it gave me a chance to warm up all my cold muscles.

That morning I ate no grain and that put me in a donkey mood.

At mid-morning I smelled horses at the same time Howard loped me down a private drive. He walked out of the stables with oats in my backpack/feedbag. Howard took off my luggage and saddle, placed the grain on the ground for me then plopped down beside me to watch me eat. After polishing off the grain, I moved on to the grass in the yard. Do I write too much about food? If I do, I won't make any apologies. Since I was the one traveling 25 miles everyday, it was all I could think about. Even on mornings when I started out with a full stomach-- having consumed 20 pounds of grain and 15 pounds of hay-I knew that being fed was never a sure thing. After the fiasco of Georgia, Howard tried hard, and succeeded in finding me grain. However, each day was a little different and always uncertain.

A mile west of my brunch I nearly got us killed. I was loping on the westbound shoulder when two horses popped out on the rise next to a house.

Seeing my fellow equines, I stopped and whinnied "Hi." They answered. Howard was patient with this stopping and chatting. Suddenly two little creatures ran over the hill and stopped in front of the horses. I wasn't sure what they were and backed up as fast as I could. We were halfway across the highway, when I heard the scream of car tires sliding on the asphalt. At the same moment I felt Howard's spurs dig deep into my flanks, causing a very sharp pain. I leaped forward in reaction to the pain and then felt the whoosh of air as a pickup just missed my tail. Being blind on the right side, I had not seen the westbound pickup truck.

Howard leaped off me and tried to lead me into the yard. The creatures were still scaring me and I did not budge.

"Misty, Misty, it's two goats!" Howard screamed at me.

I wanted to get away from those two little creatures. Howard led me down the road, until we no longer saw the horses and goats. I trembled from what had happened. Howard's voice changed to a soft tone. He stroked my neck and shoulders and told me that everything was fine.

"You're okay girl," he crooned. "You just reacted like a horse is supposed to, you know, run away from unknown creatures. Not your fault Misty."

After five minutes he mounted up and off we flew for a mile or so. I ran off the adrenaline.

Once again the shoulders and ditches disappeared. Howard dismounted and walked over a mile but then remounted.

"Sorry girl," he said. "I know the asphalt is hard on you."

The whole afternoon was miserable as every step followed the unforgiving asphalt. Howard walked almost half the distance, which did help. He had done an about face on his approach to the trip. He was now doing everything possible to look out for me. I started to like him.

At the north edge of Nolensville we trotted up a driveway. I smelled equine despite the stiff north wind. As darkness fell I enjoyed a nice stall at the vet clinic. Howard brought grain and hay before they locked me in for the night. A few hours later I heard his special whistle, "pesssaar, pessaar." I whinnied back at him.

"Good night, Misty," he yelled through the locked door.

Before dawn the doors opened while I was still sleeping on the floor. Howard entered my stall as I woke up.

"Easy girl," Howard said. "No need to get up just yet."

Howard knelt down and stroked my neck, withers and then played with my big ears. I heard the other horses eating their breakfast and that stirred me to rise up on all fours.

Howard sighed, "Okay, okay, Misty. I'll get you some breakfast."

I chowed down on the grain and more hay while I watched him put away his tent and stuff the cantle bag.

As suddenly as they disappeared yesterday, good shoulders reappeared. We made good time as we loped and walked our way northward. By mid-morning I knew we were entering an urban area. "WELCOME TO NASHVILLE" the sign read.

The sunny, mild day grew busy with traffic. The two-lane road became four then five lanes as we approached the city. Lunch was a bit tricky because Howard had me ride into the drive-through of a fast food joint. Little boys and girls pointed up at us and waved. I saw Howard waving back while he collected his food and drink.

Dismounting, he led me to the sidewalk where he sat down on the grass and ate. I munched on the thick, green grass next to the busy highway.

Afterwards Howard walked half the distance as we traveled through the southern part of the city. Late in the afternoon he stopped at a field of lush grass, stripped off my saddle and let me munch in the sun. After a half-hour I heard the sweet sound of a diesel motor and looked up to see a pickup truck stopping. Howard and the driver chatted for a few minutes and I saw Howard grab his blue backpack. That's always a good sign. Sure enough, the woman put two scoops of grain in the backpack and I was soon munching on sweet feed. The woman took off as I attacked the grain.

"Good news Misty," Howard said. "The woman has a barn not far from here, even though she lives in the middle of the city."

We loped off a few minutes later and after five minutes turned into a subdivision. Howard led me up a driveway, through the backyard and into a small barn tucked away into a hill. I made myself comfy in the stall as Howard dumped in grain and hay.

"Misty, isn't this great?" Howard said. "Here we are in the middle of a city and an equestrian found us with a barn no less. After a shower and dinner I'll be sleeping in her horse trailer."

Hours later Howard emerged from the house, gave me a scoop of grain and headed for the horse trailer.

Before dawn Howard fed me breakfast. As the golden sun rose over the little hill, he led me back to the main, four-lane road. Howard stopped at a restaurant along the busy highway for his breakfast, tying me to a telephone pole. The grass was good and the rush hour traffic did not bother me. Howard put my saddle and gear off to one side. After 15 minutes I stepped on my rein, breaking it. I just kept munching, though I started moving further and further away from the pole.

"Pessrrrsss, pessrrsss," Howard whistled, causing me to look up to see where he was. "Hey girl, what are doing? You broke your rein didn't you?"

Howard complained in a mock voice. I knew he wasn't mad at me. He took the rein, brought me back to the pole and retied me. After he finished his breakfast, he took out his knife tool and fixed the reins.

Two guys with a TV camera stopped by before we left breakfast. The camera guy filmed me eating grass, Howard mounting up and various other things. We didn't go very far that hour but Howard seemed to enjoy himself.

"Hey Misty," Howard said. "You are going to be a star of the local news tonight." If being on the news means better food and shoulders, I was all for it.

A few miles outside the city the shoulders and ditches disappeared for several hours. Ughh! Asphalt is not my friend. Late in the afternoon we stopped for the day, when Howard found a riding arena. After he pitched camp, he led me to a lush, grassy knoll overlooking the highway. He let me munch for three hours by moonlight. It wasn't as great as grain but it did fill me up.

It had been a short, 15-mile day so I was still awake, when a police car drove in and put his spotlight on Howard's tent. "Hello!" blared the car's loudspeaker. A few moments later, I saw Howard's hand come out of the tent, holding and waving his police retirement badge. The officer exited the patrol car and Howard stuck his head out to talk. After a few minutes the police officer drove away and Howard's snoring again cut through the bright, still night.

"You will not believe what happened last night Misty," Howard told me the next morning as he saddled me up. "The officer received a call from someone worried I was going to start living at the riding arena. I assured the officer that we would leave this morning and never, ever stay here again. What kind of a donkey dunce would call the cops with such an idea? Oh well, the officer was nice and I got back to sleep okay."

The shoulders were hit or miss all day. Early in the afternoon a woman in a pickup stopped along side us.

"Would you like some lunch, cowboy?" she asked Howard.

"Yes ma'am," Howard said. "That would be nice of you."

She gave Howard directions and 20 minutes later we trotted into her driveway. He stripped me and led me to a small paddock. Minutes later I was eating senior horse feed and hay. Howard vanished into the mobile home.

During Howard's next walking time he told me how amazing it was that people trusted him so much.

"Is it my white cowboy hat or your charm Misty that generates so much trust?" Howard asked.

The answer was clear to me. His hat was now more brown that white. I reasoned that it was the combination of man and his horse that opened all the doors. How could a man riding his horse across America be a bad person? The one key note I found on this ride across America was the unbridled friendliness of most people we met. They fell over themselves to help us. It was like they saw in Howard and me a quest that they too would love to be experiencing. But for some reason or other, they hadn't found the courage or time to make their own ride. Nonetheless, they saw Howard as someone fulfilling his dreams, which, in Howard's own way, he gave strangers the gift of the possibilities for their dreams.

I was finishing the hay, when Howard re-emerged to tack me up. Howard waved to the woman as we loped off onto westbound US 70.

Horses and humans appreciate a good lunch. The flat terrain made for an easy day on the trail. As evening approached, we stopped at the feed store in Dickson.

"Got any broken bags?" Howard asked the clerk.

"I think we do," she said. "I will be right back."

The clerk vanished through a door. I saw the half-full bag of grain and started to salivate. Howard was not successful in trying to pay for the grain. He tipped his cowboy hat to the woman as we trotted off.

Dickson was a small city but it was now past sundown. Howard had a worried look on his face because I know he did not like to travel at night. A few moments later, I saw an old house with a "For Sale" sign in the front yard. It looked deserted and Howard confirmed that when we walked to the back. After stripping me, he hooked me up to a clothesline in the back yard. He put grain in my bag and dinner was served!

"I don't think anyone can see us with those trees blocking out the view Misty," Howard whispered. "I think we will be okay here. Just don't jerk hard on the clothes line tonight."

He disappeared around the corner of the house, returning a few minutes later with a root beer soda. He set up his tent near me, slipped in and snored into the night air. I polished off the grain, sipped water from the bucket and fell asleep standing up.

A light sprinkle woke me up around first light. The city came to life and the sound of traffic increased. Howard had pitched camp off the main road. A few minutes later I heard the familiar sounds Howard makes when he wakes up. I nickered softly, letting him know it was time to feed me.

"Okay, miss 'gotta be fed right away," Howard cried out.

I nickered again when his head popped through the tent zipper.

"Nag, nag, nag, I'm coming," Howard said.

He grabbed my feedbag and a minute later I munched on a tasty breakfast. Whatever it takes to get fed was my motto!

Howard walked through the town, stopping at a café on the west edge for his eggs and coffee. He spent an hour eating today. Knowing how much he likes to meet people, he spent half the time trying to solve world problems with the locals.

The weather grew sunny and not too hot today. Rolling hills were pretty and easy on my body. After two hours I spied some water in a ditch and headed for it.

"No girl, that looks bad," Howard said. "I'll find you some good water."

A mile or so later he walked me up the driveway of someone's house. A man walked out and Howard asked to pour some water into my collapsible bucket. The man led us out back to the hose near the clothesline. Howard was filling my bucket full, when something on the ground streaked between the trees. I backed up fast, trying to get away. I felt the pressure of something catching the saddle horn but it did not slow me down.

"Easy girl, easy girl," Howard's voice sang out.

I stopped trying to figure out what kind of creature had jumped out. Now I noticed that there were white lines lying on the ground leading up to my saddle.

'Uh oh, I broke something', I thought.

"I am really sorry sir," Howard said. "She tore down your clothesline. How much do I owe you?"

The man looked at the damage: "She didn't really break anything. It will just take 10 minutes to put it back up. No big deal."

Howard placed the water bag down and I gulped six quarts. Howard led me off the property before I could break something else.

Late in the day I smelled animals coming from a building on the outskirts of a town called Waverly. It wasn't horse smells but Howard trotted us to the front door anyway. Howard ducked inside and came out smiling, holding a bag. I nickered approval because I have learned that those bags always contain some kind of grain. He filled my bag and let me eat. He stripped off the saddle and plopped down on the ground next to me.

"Sorry for the 27 mile day girl," Howard said. "We had to get to this town or I would not have eaten dinner. Now that I am walking 10 miles a day, I need to keep up my strength, too. Have you noticed I have lost about 15 pounds since we started?"

I had noticed his weight being less and it was appreciated. After I finished, Howard poured a generous portion into the feed bag, taking the rest of the bag back into the vet clinic.

Howard trotted me on the town's bypass stopping at the west edge. Since he has two eyes, he saw the baseball field 200 yards off the right side of the roadway. He walked me over and after closing all the gates and putting some benches over some other openings, let me loose. I rolled in the sand between two white canvas bags separated by dirt before attacking the right field grass. I like to keep an eye on my friend and I saw him walking back across the street to a 24-hour café as the sun kissed the western sky.

Two hours later I saw him cross the street. Luckily horses have excellent night vision. His long absence had disturbed me and I let him know it. I whinnied several times.

"Sorry girl but I was hungry and well you know, I got to talking," he said as he grabbed my feed bag and put it in front of me.

Food! There is no better peace offering for a horse than food. 'Okay' I thought, you are forgiven, as I chewed on the sweet feed.

Before dawn Howard offered me a breakfast of grain, and then went back to the café across the street. The soft rolling hills made for easy going through the day. After lunch we came to a big bridge. The sign read "Tennessee River." Howard did not tense up for this one maybe because it was four lanes and even had a breakdown lane. We slowed to a trot and started over the bridge. Wanting to know everything, I turned my head to the right to verify the good road condition. It was then I noticed in the river near the shore two areas where the water bubbled up. Strange! After eight minutes we stepped off the bridge and onto the long causeway.

We had been on the road for a week now and I was hoping Howard would find a place for a rest day. I felt pretty good but still, a day off would be nice.

The rain started shortly after crossing the big bridge. I accepted it. Howard keeps us going no matter what. We were soon drenched. The spray coming off the tires of the passing big trucks irritated my eye. Westward we plodded. We were riding through Huntingdon, when a man called out to Howard.

"Hey cowboy," he said. "You and your horse look like you could use a place to stay tonight."

"That's a fact mister," Howard said. "If you're offering, we are accepting." "Okay, I'll go back and hook up my trailer. You just keep going and we'll find you on the side of the road," the man replied.

"Thanks a bunch," Howard said as the man drove away.

We rode a couple of more miles before I heard that sweet sound of a diesel motor slowing down behind us. Fifteen minutes later I was in a stall with a bucket of grain, lots of water and lots of good hay. Way to go Howard! Half an hour later Howard came over to me. Since he didn't stink, I knew he had showered. Sometimes, I wish he would keep a barnyard away from me!

"Good news girl," Howard said. "Gene offered to let us stay here for a rest day. We need a day off plus it is going to rain all day tomorrow. What do you think?"

I grabbed a mouthful of grain, looked up and gave Howard my 'let's stay here a month' look. To my way of thinking, it had been a done-deal question.

Later in the evening Howard dropped more oats in my bucket, plus more hay.

"Night Misty. You deserve the rest."

He has learned what it takes to keep my weight up and me happy. Thank goodness for his growing horse sense!

Early the next morning Howard fed me breakfast with his spurs on. Spurs always mean it is a riding day. 'Oh no', I thought, he promised me a day off.

"Hey girl, you stay here and enjoy the stall," Howard said. "Gene and I are going to ride his horses in a nearby state park. I have never been on a gaited horse and I can't pass up this opportunity. We'll be back late this afternoon."

I went back to my oats thinking what a crazy cowboy Howard was to go ride a horse in a drizzle on his day off.

Before sunrise, Howard put me in Gene's trailer for the ride back to the highway. We started the overcast day right where we stopped two days ago. Gene wished us luck as he drove back to his ranch. We took the bypass around Huntingdon and headed north again along Tennessee 22. The rolling hills flattened out to a plain as the sun peeked through the clouds. It became a perfect spring day. We galloped and walked while the miles added up. Howard saved some grain from Gene's barn, which made for a good eating day. Howard stopped around mid-day, stripped my gear and let me munch grass on the shoulder of the road. He only left my bridle on. Since he was sitting down 20-30 feet away, he trusted me not to run into traffic. Since I had my tail dusted by that truck last week, I understand that the roadway is no place for a horse. Besides, I had not seen a lion or one those alligators yet.

Late in the afternoon we rode the bypass around Dresden. On the north edge of town, I smelled horses as Howard crossed the roadway into the ranch. Howard stepped inside the saddle shop for a minute. His big smile coming out told me we were staying there for the night. After being stripped of gear, Howard led me to a small turnout area near the barn.

"I'm sleeping in the tack room Misty," he said. "You'll be here by yourself and should be fine."

It was best to be by myself. When other horses are in the same paddock, they take advantage of my blind side to bite and kick me. Tonight I was able to socialize with other horses over the fence and sleep by myself.

"Misty, Edsel and I are going to breakfast," Howard said. "We'll be back about the time you finish your grain and hay."

Eating grain and hay for two days made me a happy camper before starting a 25-mile day.

The flat land made an easy morning. Howard stopped in the middle of Martin for lunch. He had to park me across the street. As usual, he came out every five minutes or so to check on me. Halfway through his lunch he moved me to another pole so I could have more grass. How thoughtful! He is turning out to be a very real friend. A man took some pictures of Howard and me. I wasn't sure what this was about.

"He was a reporter, Misty," Howard said. "He is going to write a story of our trip for the local paper."

It seemed like every couple of days a person wrote a bunch of notes and took our picture.

Late in the afternoon we took another bypass and shortly thereafter I read a big sign which read: "WELCOME TO KENTUCKY." I didn't know how far it was to Oregon but at least we were making progress. Toward evening it did not look good for finding someone to stay with. When I had about given up hope, I smelled lots of scents.

Howard led me up a short driveway where scents overwhelmed my nostrils. I smelled equine, bovine, chickens, rabbits, geese, ducks and others I did not recognize. Howard tied me up and knocked on the door. After several tries without a reply, his dejected face told me that we would be camping in the woods. He led me down the driveway, hopping on as we came to the highway.

We had only gone 200 yards, when a small pickup pulled in behind us.

"Hey cowboy," the man said. "Was that you knockin' on my door?"

"Yes, that was us," Howard replied.

"Come on back," he said. "You and your horse can spend the night."

"Much obliged mister. My name is Howard and this is my partner, Misty."

I spent the night in a strange area, which was not a stall and not a bedroom but a combination of the two. A horse was my neighbor as were dozens of birds, rabbits, cows and other assorted farm creatures. I was well fed with a roof over my head and that was all that mattered to this Trans-continental horse!

CHAPTER 3—KENTUCKY BLUE GRASS

Howard had us on the road shortly after sunrise.

"Misty, you will not believe what I did last night," Howard said. "I used a blowgun shooting darts at a target. Adron was a professional trapper and had this huge collection of traps and animal pelts. I had never seen anything like it. He told me stories of trapping beaver in cottonmouth infested waters while shooting snakes left and right. It was incredible!"

I had never seen Howard get that excited about someone he stayed with.

The 18-mile day flowed easily over flat terrain or soft, rolling hills. The shoulders provided firm traction yet soft enough to be easy on my joints. Lunch time in Clinton produced another newspaper interview for Howard. He tied me up to a power pole right next to the roadway. I felt so comfortable I took a load off my legs by lying down. It was the first time I had laid down during lunch since we started. My joints thanked me and I planned to do it again.

Howard immediately came out to check on me, when he saw me on the grass.

"You okay Misty?" he asked as he stroked my neck and shoulders.

I nickered softly as he headed back to his lunch.

Later, just north of town I became thirsty and tired. I headed for some puddles in the ditch.

"Okay, girl. I understand," Howard said.

A few minutes later Howard knocked on the back door of a house on the side of the road. A gray-haired woman looked through the glass, saw us and opened the door.

"What are you doing?" she asked Howard.

"We're riding across America and Misty is thirsty. Could we trouble you to let us use your hose?" Howard replied.

"Of course! You need a bucket?" she inquired.

"No ma'am. I have a portable bucket," Howard said as he moved over to the hose.

Howard had dropped the reins on the ground, which I knew meant I should not move. Howard called that being 'ground tied'. I was confident he would return with the bucket full of water and he did.

"Would you like a sandwich and some coffee cowboy?" she asked Howard.

Howard told her we had just had lunch but he did accept the coffee. The frail, old woman and Howard ended up at a picnic table for 10 minutes talking. Howard thanked her for the hospitality and conversation, as he hopped on my back.

"Anytime," she replied. "You are always welcome."

"Do you believe how trusting she was Misty?" Howard said. "There she was all alone, 80 years old and she just treated me like I was her son. Of course, I know it's because you Misty girl are with me that she opened her door and came outside. You generate trust with people and I just happen to be with you."

I snorted loudly to let the cowboy know that it was his horse people trusted and liked, not him so much. Howard laughed after I snorted.

"Good timing, girl. Or did you understand what I just said?"

Toward evening I heard that distinctive throaty noise of a diesel slow down behind us. 'YES!' I thought. Howard reined me up and hopped off to meet the man exiting the truck.

"My name is Larry and you look like you have come a long ways cowboy," he declared.

"My name is Howard, this is Misty and you're right. We've been on the road about two months, since we left Savannah, Georgia," Howard replied.

"Holy smokes. Savannah to here. You must be loco but then I have done some crazy things in my life too. Use some grain?" he asked.

"Thanks Larry, much appreciated," Howard replied as Larry handed him half a bag.

"Know anywhere we can camp tonight?" Howard asked.

"I live too far from here but there are a couple of abandoned trailers just up the road on the left. I bet you can camp there without a problem," Larry advised.

I chewed on the grain the whole time Larry and Howard were ratchet-jawing. After I finished, Howard rode me another mile or so and pulled into the drive where five old trailers were falling apart. Howard stripped me off and tied me up short, before he went across the street to talk to the people and fetch me a bucket of water. Upon returning, he set up his tent behind one trailer. He led me to the tall grass near the highway and let me loose. He sat down in the grass between the highway and me. It had been a nice easy day.

I'd been munching for an hour, when a car pulled up near us.

"Hey cowboy. Where you from? You hungry? I have an extra double cheese, double bacon burger here," the young woman driver asked Howard.

"A Texas cowboy is always hungry and I appreciate you thinking about me," Howard replied.

After she drove off, Howard wolfed down the burger and polished it off with a big drink out of his water bottle.

"People are just so nice Misty, sometimes I can't believe it."

Howard hooked me up to the picket line well after dark and ducked into his tent. I was asleep on my feet, when another car pulled in near us. I nickered loudly at the intrusion. I could see it was a police car and I thought, 'I hope they don't kick us out now, five hours till dawn'. A man and woman stepped out of the patrol car, shining a flashlight on Howard's tent.

"Hey cowboy, you awake?" the man asked.

"Yes sir, am I in trouble for sleeping here?" Howard asked.

"No, no you're okay. I'm the sheriff, this is my wife Margaret, we heard about you and your horse. We are just being nosey," he admitted.

"That Pinto is Misty, my name is Howard, I'm a retired cop and I normally hang my hat in Fort Worth, Texas," Howard informed them.

"Well, go back to sleep. Sorry to bother you," the sheriff apologized as he got back in the squad car.

Howard's snoring minutes later told me he had no problem with the last command.

I finished off the last of the oats at breakfast and we headed out at first light. Howard stopped for breakfast in Bardwell. He short tied me up in the parking lot in a spot that had no grass and I stood on a sidewalk. Sometimes there is just not a good place to park a horse for 30 minutes.

As Howard saddled me back up, he laughed to himself.

"Misty, we need to gallop on out of here," Howard said. "An old woman in there accused me of abusing you and I couldn't convince her otherwise. I think she might call the animal protection people on us."

'Gallop out of here?' I thought. How fast does he think I can go? Faster than a car? He led me out of town so I realized he was just joking.

North of town Howard did ask me how I was. Since leaving Chattanooga, I had no complaints. We had been taken in many times. I had been receiving good amounts of grain and grass, and the hills were not too steep. Except for a few bad miles without shoulders, it had been good traveling. Howard had kept pretty much to the lope two miles, get off and walk one routine. That meant that he was never on my back more than three hours per day. Except when he carried some grain for me, the 14 pounds of cantle bag was all I had to carry. I had no complaints. The cowboy was taking care of his horse.

In the afternoon we entered a forest that stretched for miles and encountered some good-sized hills. Late in the afternoon we rounded a curve and I saw a big, blue bridge ahead. Howard stopped and checked all my gear before proceeding.

"Girl, we are about to ride on a high sidewalk in the sky," Howard said. "You have the right stuff to take us over. Trust your instincts and allow the courage you have to carry us safely over."

I placed my trust in Howard and knew in my heart that I could overcome any obstacle. At first the narrow bridge was over land but moments later I saw this huge river 150 feet below us. My eye got big as could be. This was incredible! I was so far off the ground and over water, I couldn't believe it. Where the pavement ended, a short steel girder acted as a barrier. I felt the tension build in Howard's seat as we moved over the water.

"Easy girl. No problem for you," Howard called out.

The wind was light and Howard had no trouble keeping me in the middle of our lane. The traffic built up behind us but no one blew their horn. That was good because I was scared. If we made a mistake, we would both die. Howard kept me at a steady trot and all went well. After 10 minutes we left the bridge and I tried to break into a gallop. The adrenaline levels were making me bounce up and down. We turned into a park to our left. As soon as we got off the pavement, I broke into a dead gallop as the adrenaline flowed through my veins. Man was that a scary a bridge. I raced 1000 yards, slowing down only because I was running out of land. Howard forced me into a circle, trying to slow me down. Finally I stopped and Howard hopped off.

"You were great Misty. You took that bridge over the Ohio River like you did it everyday. You're the best," Howard exclaimed.

I was still pretty pumped up and blowing hard as Howard led me to where two great rivers converged.

"This is called The Point, Misty," Howard said. "Here the Ohio and Mississippi Rivers come together and head towards the Gulf of Mexico. Pretty impressive, eh?"

The combined river must be a mile wide. It was a lot of water; speaking of which, I was thirsty.

Howard must have read my mind because he led me over near a trailer, stripped my gear and brought me a bucket of cool water. After I gulped the whole thing, he fetched another one. Howard set up his tent and then led me to some grass. I had only been munching a few minutes, when Howard quickly led me back to the picket line he had strung up on one tree between two branches. As he hooked me up I noticed the northern sky had gone black and the wind was starting to pickup. I saw Howard scurry into his tent as I realized I was about to get soaked and windblown. Sure enough, five minutes later the thunderstorm slammed into the park with 50 mile an hour winds and rain. I turned my butt into the wind-driven rain so the stinging only hit mostly there. Ow, ouch, ow, oww, ouch as the rain lashed my butt and part of my flank and head. Darn! Why can't I have a tent?

After 30 brutal minutes the wind dropped to near zero, though the rain continued. Howard popped out of the tent with his rain gear on and led me to some grass. An hour later a man drove up, said a few words to Howard and left. Twenty minutes later as we headed back to our campsite, the same man drove up again. This time he stepped out and came over to me. I saw he had a bag and I was hoping…Yes, I could smell carrots! He fished out a big one and let me bite off a hunk. Five minutes later I had eaten a whole pound of carrots. Thanks mister.

"Speaking for my horse, it was awful nice of you to bring back the carrots. They are her favorite," Howard said.

The old man replied, "I'm a volunteer who takes care of the park and I used to own a horse. How far you two going?"

"Coast to coast, from Georgia to Oregon," Howard replied. The man let out a long whistle.

"Good luck then," he said as he got went back to his van.

"Thanks for everything sir," Howard responded.

The tugboat engines on the Ohio River roared all night. But after a few hours, I was tired enough to fall asleep.

CHAPTER 4—LAND OF LINCOLN

No breakfast for me as Howard led us back to the water's edge. After we left The Point, I spied a sign: "WELCOME TO CAIRO, ILLINOIS." We rode for a few minutes before Howard stopped for breakfast. He tied me up across the street in a vacant lot with lots of grass. After breakfast Howard smiled as he told me that we were not riding through town. We traveled two city streets, before cutting between two yards. We charged up a big mound of dirt that had a road on top of it. We walked that dike for the next seven miles. With its hard dirt and no traffic it was the best place to ride since we started.

Later in the afternoon, a woman drove up and stopped.

"Hi, my name is Mitzy," she said. "You hungry? I brought some turkey and potatoes. Sorry I don't have anything for your horse."

Howard ate the food while I munched on the grass. Howard thanked her for the food and we again headed north on Route 3.

I noticed Howard limping and though he was still walking his one-mile in three, it concerned me. Later in the afternoon it worsened, the limp now being very pronounced.

"Misty, I may have to ride you more," Howard said. "My big toe is killing me and I don't know why. That lady Mitzy told me there was a park south of Olive Branch and I think we will make it a short day."

Less than an hour later, we strolled into a nice, well-maintained park with a baseball field, picnic tables and jungle gym for the kids. Howard placed all his gear under the roof of the picnic area and turned me loose in the ball field to eat. Mitzy drove up and soon I was eating grain. Thank you Mitzy. The terrain that day had been flat as a pancake, great shoulders and now grain for dinner and breakfast. Life was good. Later that evening I saw Mitzy return. Howard got in her car and he started eating something. I was sure he was happy because otherwise he would have had a dinner of his two emergency candy bars and water.

Soon after Mitzy left, a whole carload of girls showed up as Howard was about to crawl into his sleeping bag. The ladies produced a bag and it looked like Howard had a little more food that night. They did give Howard a big blanket that he took back to his sleeping bag. The wind came up strong just after they left, blowing away anything not tied down.

A couple of hours later yet another car drove up into the park. I watched it draw nearer and stop. Yeooowww! A spotlight was put in my eye and I couldn't see anything. I snorted and whinnied loudly in protest. Do something Howard!

I heard Howard's voice cut the night, "Is there a problem officer?"

"Your horse acts like he is about to break loose," a man said. "You better do something quick."

"Take the spotlight out of her eye and she will calm down," Howard replied.

The light shifted to Howard's head as the voice in the car yelled, "Be sure you clean up the horse poop in the morning, okay?"

I did calm down right away without that awful light in my eye. I could tell it was a police car by the overheads.

"You have my word as a retired police officer that I will clean up her poop in the morning," Howard promised.

The car drove away. The wind howled all night with some intermittent rain. I didn't sleep well that night.

An overcast sky greeted us the next morning as we pushed northward. I saw that Howard limped worse than yesterday. He kept walking every third mile but he was slowing down which was not a good sign. Around noon I saw a pickup pull in behind us.

"Hi, how's it going?" the man asked.

"We're doing okay," Howard replied.

"I have some oats for your horse, if you can use them," he said. "By the way, my name is Clyde."

"I'm Howard, nice to meet you and yes, thanks for the oats," Howard replied.

Howard filled my bag with oats and I dove in. Clyde and Howard chatted for the next 20 minutes.

The land stayed flat and we made good time, except when Howard was walking. We were loping along, when suddenly my left rear ankle was on fire. Something was biting me with every stride! I stopped abruptly and refused to move. Howard jumped down and asked me to be still. 'No problem', I thought. Howard took out his handy tool and carefully cut the wire around my ankle. There was only a little blood.

Howard exhaled deeply as he showed me the piece of barbwire, which had become wrapped around my ankle. It had been the little barbs which had been 'biting' me. Howard placed the barbwire in my pack to dispose of later.

"Stuff happens Misty," he said.

We made a turn onto Route 146, rode a short distance and stopped in a small town. The sign said "CAMPING" and Howard led us there. We had never stayed at a real campground before. It was still early afternoon, when Howard stripped my gear.

He gave me a long shower, massaging all my muscles with his strong hands. It felt great. He let me eat the grass near the tent for an hour. As I lay down to rest, he stood by. I wanted to fall asleep, since I had not slept at all last night. Sleeping on the ground was an option, only when another horse watches over me. Could I trust Howard to be a good sentinel? I thought back on the last two months and how he had always tried his best to take care of me. Sure, I could trust him with my life. I rolled over onto the soft earth, lay my head on the grass and promptly fell into a deep sleep. An hour later I woke up and Howard still stood where I last saw him. I stayed another 15 minutes on the grass, feeling lazy in the setting sun. Howard came over, said "Hi," and stroked my neck, withers and flank.

"Did you have a good nap, Misty?" Howard said. "Was last night miserable or what? I wish I could have brought you under the shelter but there was no way. And that cop! I couldn't believe what a muffin head he was to put the spotlight in your eye."

I popped up, shook and let Howard hook me up to the picket line. I nickered as he left the park to eat at the restaurant across the street. I watched him come out the door every few minutes to check on me. He was still limping but it did not seem as bad, when he returned an hour later. He checked my water before going into his tent. Indeed, he was my friend and I trusted him with my life. Little did I know that the next day would put that trust to the ultimate test of the ride.

CHAPTER 5—SHOW ME STATE

After Howard ate breakfast across the street, we headed out. We had gone a few yards, when I saw the tall bridge looming in front of us. When we neared the bridge, Howard stopped and re-checked my cinch, hooves, tie downs and bridle. He stepped in front of me, looked me in the eye and stroked my face.

"Misty we are about to take another high sidewalk over a river," Howard said. "I won't lie to you. The bridge is going to be very dangerous. It is old, narrow and in a bad state of repair. It only has two lanes, there are no safety devices, no breakdown lane and if we make a mistake, it is 150 feet to the Mississippi River. I have great faith that you and I can ride over this bridge. As we cross over the bridge, we will have completed 1000 miles on our journey. We will be Long Riders. I am so proud of you. Let's go girl."

Howard put his left boot in the stirrup and swung into the saddle. After the traffic cleared, he urged me into a trot and we stepped onto the bridge. Immediately I knew we stood far above the river. I glanced through the old, rusting, gray steel girders and saw that the river was angry. The wind formed white caps as it tried to push the water back up stream. The crosswind howled at 40 miles per hour, directly out of the south. As the traffic built up behind us, I felt Howard's tension in his seat and legs. He had a reason. Where the asphalt ended, a steel girder stood three feet high and then nothing but air and the river far below. As I moved my head to the right to compensate for no eye, I spotted holes where the asphalt met the girder, which were big enough to put my hoof through. Howard would have to help me avoid those holes or surely we would fall over and tumble into the river. The strong wind caused the bridge to sway a little.

Howard gave me good leg cues to keep me in the middle of our lane. However sometimes the wind blew harder and we stepped close to those holes on the edge. Several times Howard over-compensated and pushed me too far to the left and I was afraid we would be hit by the oncoming traffic. After a couple of minutes my nerves jangled inside my head. I stopped and pooped and didn't quite know what to do. What am I doing here? Where were my friends, Texas, my comfortable stall, good hay and steady feed?

Howard's soothing voice came into my ears, "Misty, Misty. You're okay girl. You can do this. I know you can. Just look straight ahead and take the rest of this sidewalk in the sky at a trot."

His voice soothed my frazzled nerves. I moved out at a trot. Howard's fingers were on my withers as constant reminders of his presence. I noticed drivers making a big "O" with their mouths as they passed us. I guessed that had never seen a horse trotting over that bridge. Thank goodness nobody honked their horns. We were nearing the end of the bridge when despite Howard's best efforts, I lost my confidence again and stopped. I started walking in place and tossing my head in fear and indecision.

"It's okay Misty. Almost there. Just move forward and we are done in a minute."

Howard's voice drifted into my ears and gave me the courage to go on. I started forward again and indeed, we stepped off the bridge in less than a minute.

A sign read, "Welcome to Missouri: The Show Me State."

As soon as we left the bridge, Howard reined me onto the shoulder, waving a thank you to the patient drivers. He directed me onto a dirt two-track used by the construction workers who were building a new bridge. Open road in view, without asking for permission, I broke into a dead gallop.

Howard screamed, "Yeehaa," and yelled at the top of his lungs like a cowboy who had just arrived in Dodge City after a cattle drive. I raced as fast as my legs could run, until the dirt ended a quarter mile away. The adrenaline rushed through my body and I trembled with fear and excitement.

Howard stripped me, let me eat and gave me time to calm down. Most special to me was the huge hug, kiss and repeated "Thank you" for my courage. Looking back at the bridge, I could scarcely believe I had trotted over it. It was at that moment I understood what it meant to be a Long Rider horse.

Working as a team, we could take our Long Rider anywhere; do anything against all odds or opinions. Out of the tens of millions of horses in the world, we were of the few hundred who had proven we had 'the right stuff' to go the distance. Howard and I were now one with the road and the bond between us as seamless and strong as a steel I-beam.

Outside the city, we stopped briefly at a restaurant before heading north on US 61. I loped hard the next two miles. I still felt the need to shake the feelings from that bridge. Howard had to rein me up hard to stop me. When he walked, I noticed his limp was almost gone. Whatever the problem had been, it was leaving him fast.

We chewed up 23 miles before stopping for the night. At the north end of Union Town, Howard received permission to camp on a triangle of land near the highway. While Howard pitched his tent, a man and his young son stopped by. After they talked a few minutes, Howard came over with hay.

"Misty, Glenn has invited me to his house for supper," Howard said. "Here is a bit of dinner for you. Will you be okay by yourself? Don't let anybody steal you!"

The hay was good quality and I was munching when they drove off and still munching when they returned. Since he had shaved and didn't stink, I could tell that he ate a meal and took a hot shower. He did look extra somber. He told me that Glenn had cancer and the outlook was not good.

"It is important to live each day to the fullest, Misty girl," he said. "You never know how much future you have."

Glenn had appeared to be 10 years younger than Howard and his grave disease made me pause.

As customary, Howard moved us onto the road at sunrise. I was glad because the days were getting warmer and it was more comfortable for me to put on the bulk of a day's miles in the coolness of the morning. We had traveled only an hour or so, when I smelled some equines near the road. Howard noticed the mules also and pulled into the driveway. In no time I was chewing on sweet feed. The man let down the tailgate of the pickup and both of them plopped down to continue their conversation. 'Oh good', I thought, they will chat for at least 30 minutes, knowing Howard. While Howard and the man solved the world's problems, I consumed 10 pounds of sweet feed.

"Whoa, that's enough Misty girl," Howard said. "I don't want you to colic."

He snatched the food away. At least he poured a lunch portion into my backpack for later.

The rolling, curvy road made for good traveling and well before sundown, we arrived at St. Mary's. Howard hooked me up to the picket line, while he ate at the local restaurant. Then it was my turn for grazing next to the roadway, followed by grain out of the backpack. After I was all done, Howard surprised me with a bunch of little carrot chunks.

"All for you girl, compliments of the waitress at the restaurant," Howard said. "I told her about you and a minute later she gave me this bag of carrots."

Howard fed me the chunks one at a time, extending my eating pleasure. Are people nice to horses or what?

Moving out at daybreak without breakfast, we made good time on smooth, wide shoulders. The sky threatened rain that never came. The flat river flood plain gave way to rolling, tree filled hills that were easy to run up and down. Howard stopped and asked someone in a pickup where a horse ranch was. A few miles later, we loped into a long driveway.

"Anyone home?" Howard yelled.

His shouting caught the attention of a few horses in a turnout pen but no response.

"I don't feel good about this Misty but I am going to feed you without permission," Howard said.

Howard led me over to a small barn. He put three scoops of grain in my blue bag and left a dollar on the table. Brunch was mighty tasty.

Leaving the ranch, I stopped and pooped but only one or two stools came out. Ten minutes later the same thing happened. And again, and again.

"Misty, what is wrong with you?" Howard asked.

He grimaced as he examined my stools for any obvious problems. My stomach had suffered the 'feel-me-no-goods' since last night. I was strong and wasn't sick, so Howard kept us going, though he examined my poop each time that day. The queasy feeling diminished as the day went by and by the following day I felt fine.

A couple of hours later we stopped for lunch at a Pizza Hut in St. Genieve. As usual, Howard tied me to the wooden poles, stripped me and went inside.

Being tired, I laid down on the soft grass immediately and, feeling sleepy, I flopped my head over on the grass and fell fast asleep.

Minutes later Howard's voice floated into my dream...Misty it's me, Howard. I know you're okay but the people in the restaurant think you are dead... I woke up as he began to stroke my neck and withers. I raised my head and looked towards the restaurant. Sure enough, there must have been 20 noses glued to the windows looking at me. Howard left and I, again looking dead, fell asleep.

After lunch, two police officers stopped us and chatted with Howard a few minutes. I enjoyed the fact I could take a small break. North of Bloomsdale, Howard directed me into the parking lot of the Beacon Bar. Two patrons came out, swaying slightly and shouted at us.

"Bring your horse on into the bar and we'll buy you both a beer," one of them offered.

Howard dismounted and led me to the door, where a woman screamed at the two guys to get their sorry, drunk butts back into the bar.

"I wasn't really going to take my horse into the bar ma'am," Howard explained. "But I am looking for a place to spend the night."

The woman gave Howard directions to a nearby ranch. A half-mile later, we trotted down a long tree-lined road toward a barn.

Darkness fell as Howard stripped my gear off at a small shed and tied me to the rail of the nearby round pen. I snorted impatiently for food and water and pawed the ground. After a few seconds I hooked my leg around the rein and I couldn't move. Beating down the instinct to break loose, I waited patiently until Howard called out a few minutes later.

"Misty, you okay girl?" Howard asked.

I whinnied loudly and long, causing Howard to come at a run.

"Oh, geez girl," Howard said. "I am sorry I tied you too low. Thanks for not busting the rein. Thanks for telling me you had a problem."

Howard apologized as he untangled the rein from my front left leg. Our communications skills improved with each passing day. He led me into the round pen that was full of tall grass. The lush grass helped me forget the incident.

The owner's mother Mae McGee walked over later to see me and give Howard a cup of coffee. Howard sipped while the elderly woman described a two-week long horse trip she had taken about 70 years ago. I could see her as a young girl riding across the rural stretches of Missouri. In the soft light coming from the ranch's night light, I saw her face light up and eyes twinkle as she recounted the days of her youthful adventure.

We hit the road at the crack of dawn and made good time on the solid shoulders. Howard was walking me through the town of Festus, when another guy stepped out of bar and yelled, "What are you doing?"

Howard yelled back, "Coast to coast."

"I'll buy you a cold soda, if you tell me some stories."

Quick as he could cross the street, he tied me up at a sign in the parking lot and walked inside. I hoped he wouldn't be too long as I stood on asphalt. Ten minutes later Howard emerged and told me about a pizza he had just wolfed down. 'Great', I thought, but what about my lunch? North of town Howard stripped me and let me graze on the side of the road for an hour. He had read my mind.

The highway went from two to four lanes signaling the approach of a large city. Howard told me were going through a big chunk of a St. Louis. It would be the largest city so far on the trip.

After a short, easy ride Howard held up at a restaurant in the small town of Pevely. A few minutes later I saw a wonderful sight; a truck pulling an empty horse trailer enter the lot. I hopped in. A few minutes later I backed out and Howard led me into a barn. Ten or so of my equine pals whinnied as I came in and was put in a stall. Howard saw to it that I had all the hay and grain I wanted. After he ate dinner with the family, Howard pitched his tent in the stall next to me. About midnight the heavens opened up and it poured down hard. As the night had turned cool, I was extra happy to be in a barn that night.

I hopped back in the trailer the next morning as the rain continued. Oh great! Another day of riding in the rain with mushy ground. Howard and Don stopped at a café in Pevely for breakfast while I stayed dry in the trailer. Just as they came out, the rain stopped! Even better, the shoulders featured gravel and I felt good traction despite the heavy rain.

Around noon a man in a pickup stopped and invited us to lunch. A mile or so later Howard stripped my gear and led me into a stall. He offered me grain, some hay and water. I saw him eating his sandwiches and drinking soda pop. We both enjoyed a great lunch. I was so grateful that people, total strangers, stopped and helped us out. This ride challenged us on a physical and emotional level. I could not even imagine how horrible it would be without so many kind people opening up their barns and homes to us.

The traffic became thicker than horsehair on a winter pony as US 61 led us closer to the city. I slowed down to a trot and walk in many places. The last couple hours of the day Howard dismounted and led almost the whole time. We were stopped at some quality grass in front of a car dealership, when it began to drizzle. Howard looked up at the sky and shook his head. About that time a man in a diesel-powered truck stopped and asked if we needed a place to stay.

"Sure do," Howard replied.

The man promised to be back in an hour.

Sixty minutes later the man rolled up and I hopped into the back of the trailer from Fenton Rentals. Five miles later we pulled into a lot with trucks and other equipment. Howard led me into a huge pole barn where a bunch of guys were talking. They came over to get a close look at me. The concrete was too smooth and after slipping and nearly falling down, Howard led me back out and into the trailer. The nice man had bought a bale of hay and 50 pounds of oats. Howard filled up the trailer with those items plus water and I happily munched down.

Howard and the man drove off and returned a while later. Howard locked the gate, after the man left in the truck. He entered the trailer to give me the latest news.

"Oh Misty girl," he started. "Brian has saved our butts. He invited us to stay here tomorrow because it is going to rain and since it will be Sunday, he doesn't have any obligations. He bought me dinner and will take care of me all day tomorrow. Did you realize that Brian rented this trailer to help us out? Unbelievable! We are lucky to meet such wonderful people."

The next day I enjoyed not going anywhere. Howard took me out to stretch my legs a few times and that was all I needed. Not moving, staying dry and being well fed had become the gold standard of my existence on this crazy trip.

I was beginning to realize that I was part of what might be called an 'epic' adventure. It was the kind of trip that many people talk about, but few actually 'do' it. It takes a lot of courage to live your dreams. I had come to realize I was part of an odyssey and despite the hardships was honored and proud to be a part of it. Fate had put me in the hands of one of the few who make their dreams a reality. You only go around once in this life and being in a cramped trailer on a rainy Sunday in Missouri was the perfect speed for this horse on that day. I would not change a thing.

On the second exercise outing I saw Howard had showered and shaved. His face had become sunken and thin, and his jeans flopped in the wind. Though it seemed he was always eating, he had lost 15 pounds, which he would never gain back. Being a human, I figured he could take care of himself.

Brian trailered us back to the auto dealership and he and Howard said goodbye. The whole day Howard was only on my back for a few minutes. We entered the city's suburbs and Howard led me on the sidewalks. This was tedious because he would move me onto every tiny bit of grass or sand he could find. I know he was trying to save my shoes and protect my joints but it was annoying. After a short time he only needed to touched the reins to my neck and I moved over.

All day long people came up to pet me or gawk. I guess they didn't see a horse very often, living in the big city. Some were definitely afraid of me. Does he bite, does he kick several asked Howard. Hello, I am a she! Howard showed patience with such questions and he always corrected them that I was a she. In fact, Howard seems to brag about me being a mare instead of a gelding. I had heard enough equestrians talk to know that most preferred a gelding to ride over a mare. Whatever, Howard likes me and that is all that counts!

In the late afternoon, Howard looked for a place to camp. We stopped at a café. While Howard was checking it out, a young woman came up and engaged him in conversation. After she made a quick call on her cell phone, he broke into a big grin.

"Misty! We are lucky again," Howard said. "Stephanie is taking us to her parent's house near here to spend the night."

After we crossed the main street, Howard and Stephanie talked in a language I had never heard. For 10 minutes they baffled me with those sounds. Later he told me they were speaking French because it was her college major. A woman in a car stopped for a moment to give Howard 10 pounds of oats. Thank you!

The backyard became my home for the night. The fence was 18 inches high and there was a hot tub. Howard roped off the hot tub and lawn furniture with his lariat. Before he stepped inside, he asked me to be good and not hop the fence or touch the rope. He was concerned but I had no intentions of being mischievous. With all the grass plus oats, my tummy sang. After dinner I lay down and slept the remainder of the night.

Howard greeted me early the next morning. He talked of his big steak, baked potato and milk he enjoyed for dinner. He thanked me for being good and said he would try hard to find some grass. Howard led me all morning as we walked parallel to an expressway. He startled a homeowner when he asked for water for me. The man came out of his suburban house to pet me and I guess to make sure I was not a mirage.

In the afternoon the sun burned off the clouds that revealed a gorgeous day. I tired of the sidewalk routine but the city kept rolling out in front of us. It wasn't until late in the afternoon that Howard was able to hop up and ride a bit. During one of his walks, Howard stopped to talk to an officer. Afterwards he informed me that we would be stopping short of a tall bridge. We had to avoid something-called 'rush hour', which would get us killed.

Two miles later we loped onto a pumpkin farm called Rombach's. The owner found me hay so dinner was not bad at all. Howard slept next to me under a pavilion.

About the crack of dawn, I saw Howard move in the tent. I nickered to him that I was already awake and ready to start the day. The local rooster must have heard me because he crowed loudly. I whinnied long and hard, and soon the rooster and I screamed in stereo, a duet really.

"Misty, give it a rest," Howard said.

Apparently unable to fall back asleep, Howard emerged from his tent not looking happy.

At daybreak we set off, going a short distance to the café. He parked me on the grass near some shrubs. A few minutes later two police cars rolled into the parking lot and the officers approached me. 'Uh, oooh...what now?' I thought. Howard came out with a coffee cup in hand and greeted the two officers.

"We have a report that your horse is eating the shrubs."

"It also does seem not too safe for her to be tied up only 20 feet from the highway," the second officer said.

"As you can see she has not eaten any of the shrubs and she has been tied up like this since we left Georgia," Howard responded.

I kept eating as the three of them worked it out. Eventually, Howard returned to the café and the officers petted my neck and left.

After breakfast, Howard informed me that we had our last tall bridge to cross. We would cross the Missouri River in a few minutes. Locals said the bridge was tall but had three good lanes.

"No problem for you girl," Howard said. "You are a veteran of these bridges now."

We barely left the café, when the green, steel girders rose into view. Howard slowed me down to a trot and moved us onto the asphalt. Light traffic moved around us without slowing down. My left eye saw through the girders that the river was 150 feet below us. The barium cleats on my shoes gave me excellent traction. Howard produced only a little tension in his seat, as he stroked my neck and talked to me. I was cool and calm for the five minutes the crossing took and then the bridge was in our 'rear-view mirror'.

The morning sunshine gave way to clouds, as the expressway became a four lane, cross-traffic road. At a very busy intersection, he tied me to a pole in an area of tall grass and after filling my water bucket, went inside the restaurant for his lunch. After a few minutes I stepped on my rein and broke it, as I spotted better looking grass. I was about 30 feet from the pole and knew Howard would soon figure it out that I had broken the rein. After three minutes he came out and scolded me.

"Misty. Why did you do this? You broke your rein that I have to fix."

As he tied me back to the pole he did praise me for not crossing the road. Silly Howard. Why would I cross the road? The grass was better on this side!

The rest of the 27-mile day grew pleasant as the cloudy skies kept the temperature moderate and the softly rolling hills were a breeze to lope up and down. Near the town of Troy, Howard hopped off and led me a half mile to a big horse ranch. The woman agreed to allow us to stay in the barn. Howard put me in a stall and served up a heap of grain and hay. A steady rain began as he stayed with me awhile before putting on all his rain gear.

"Misty girl," Howard said. "The good news is that you have a dry stall and lots to eat. The bad news is that owners are not going to feed me. You rest and I will walk the mile to the Pizza Hut. Looking like a fireman with a cowboy hat, he walked out into the rain."

Upon his return, he refilled my grain bucket and made sure I was comfy before he retired to sleep in the nearby tack room. The rain beat softly on the roof of the barn all night, as I enjoyed the security and comfort of a stall. Little did I know it would be a long while before I enjoyed another such night.

The rain stopped its steady drumbeat as Howard served up my breakfast. He led me to a café where he ordered his pancakes and coffee. The cloudy, muggy day grew harsher as the rain had turned the shoulders soft and gooey. Often my hooves sank an inch or two, doubling the effort needed to cover the distance. In the early afternoon I broke out of my lope due to fatigue and Howard, bless his heart, noticed that I was tired. He stopped and talked to several people but was unable to find us a place. We ended up spending the night at a truck stop in Eola. Worse, there was nothing to tie me to.

Howard dragged a large metal thing to where his tent was set up on hard-packed gravel. He looped one rein through the metal and I endured an entire night on a three-foot short tie. I was miserable. Shortly after Howard called it a night, a light mist of water fell on me all night. What a change from the previous evening!

We left that miserable spot at daybreak. The shoulders had firmed up despite the mist, which had stopped. Howard broke for lunch in Bowling Green that had a café next to the local feed store. I felt much better as I chewed through my straight oats, switching to the good, green grass next to the sign Howard had tied me to. Howard left a few pounds in my feedbag which I later had for a snack.

The going continued to be easy on the shoulders of the four lane--US 61. We rode into the village of Frankford as the skies began to darken again. Howard dismounted and we moved from vacant lots to vacant houses, looking for grass. Near nightfall we were approached by a couple and after a few words, Howard's face lit up. Shortly thereafter, he led me through the village to a very small barn and paddock. He put some grain in a large bowl in the paddock as he turned me loose. The owner's donkey thought the grain should be his and moved into munch. I pinned my ears, warning him to stay away. Maybe the donkey was blind because a second later I struck out sideways with my left rear leg, smacking the would-be thief hard on his head. He then let me chew on the grain in peace as Howard smiled from the fence.

"Did you see that cow-kick Misty gave the donkey?" Howard inquired of his host.

"I never knew a horse could kick sideways but I just saw it," Charlie replied.

About that time a steady drizzle started which would last all night. I was well fed if wet that night.

Howard picked me up early and brought me back to the house where he had slept. He was clean-shaven and did not smell which was a bonus for me. We started out in the drizzle and the night's rain made for mud and tough going for me. Though the rain soon stopped, the footing was lousy the whole 32-mile day.

After lunch in Hannibal, we made a sharp turn to the west and began following US 36. We would travel this road 800 miles toward Denver, Colorado. Heavy construction west of Hannibal meant the shoulders were all wet and the sticky, red clay made the going tough on me. Late in the afternoon, Howard pulled up at a truck stop, which appeared to be another one without a place to put me on soft ground. Luckily, he found a large, ground level billboard, which blocked strong northwesterly winds. After bending all the nails back into the wood, he strung his picket line and tied me up. He set up his tent a few feet behind me. The flapping of his tent distracted me the whole night.

The gray, cloudy day to Shelbina was uneventful, except for a funny incident on a bridge. We had almost crossed a river when a man driving a pickup truck stopped and rolled down the window.

"Hey cowboy," he said. "You should know that horses don't like bridges and it is dangerous to ride over a bridge."

"Thanks much mister," Howard replied. "I'll keep that in mind the next time we come to a bridge."

After the man drove off Howard just could not stop laughing. We had trotted over some of the tallest, narrowest two lane bridges in the United States and now somebody tells us it's dangerous. I guess our ignorance was bliss. The encounter kept Howard smiling all day.

The next day we rode rollercoaster hills 22 miles into Macon under a cloudy and sometimes wet sky. Around noon a car stopped and Mary offered Howard a burger and drink. They chatted as I munched on the grass. Even though we had just left a café, Howard had no trouble gobbling up the food. In Macon Howard stopped at the feed mill and filled the bag to the top.

"Misty," he said. "Tomorrow is a break day. The town has a fairground and we are taking a day off."

He led me a mile to the south edge of town and parked me under the grandstands. After stripping me, he let me roam around the large, deserted grounds. I enjoyed the grass and lack of noise, cars and people.

The next day Howard walked back into town for a while. Upon his return, he let me roam about as he kept a watchful eye out for me. Though another gray sky, it was wonderful to not go anywhere for a whole day. Such breaks lifted my spirit and body. Though my body had grown into superb condition, it was hard for me to plug into 25 miles of riding everyday.

The great shoulders and soft, rolling hills of north central Missouri continued the next 22 miles to Bucklin. Howard again spoke to several people in the afternoon and when he led me down a small road off the main one, I thought we were going to have shelter. We were both disappointed. Howard put me in an outdoor arena without grass and he had to stay in an old building. I ate a full ration of grain but there was no grass. Howard slept on a table because he was afraid there were rats. He was offered real shelter but the ranch was two miles in the opposite direction.

"Misty, I would rather stick my hand in fire than go backwards," Howard said. "I hope you feel the same way."

I agreed with him. This road is too long to go backwards for any reason, even shelter. He ate six rolls and drank water for dinner. I appreciated him not carrying much food but I thought he may be overdoing it.

A cool, overcast morning made for an easy riding day. We covered 27 miles to Chillicothe. The near perfect shoulder made my task easy. Howard spotted some horses in the late afternoon and pulled up to the house. I enjoyed eight pounds of grain while Howard chatted with a couple. Surprisingly, they did not invite us to stay the night. As Howard led me out the driveway and onto the road, I saw he was discouraged.

"Sorry girl," Howard said. "No luck there. They did not offer and I am too stubborn or something to ask to spend the night in their barn."

A cool wind whipped up and I think both of us were expecting another very lousy night. I had lost my winter coat a long time ago. Like magic, this large, white barn came into view. We investigated and Howard smiled. He moved 30 old bales of hay and made a spot for me. As he let me munch near the roadway, it began to rain. We retreated to the barn, where he opened up a good bale of hay for me to eat. I saw him put two dollars on a machine where the owner would see it. Howard slept on the hay.

The next day I was a bit of a star during lunch at the Golden Corral in Chillicothe. All kinds of kids and grownups came up to pet me as I ate the grass. Howard and a former Los Angeles police officer had a long discussion next to me after which he bought Howard lunch. To make life perfect, a guy stopped by and gave me five pounds of sweet feed! We loped off and a short time later, Howard stopped to get water for me. This resulted in our invitation to spend the night at the Peterson ranch. Howard turned me loose in a 10-acre field with a small lake. I wondered around the rest of the day but after Howard pitched his tent, I stayed near him the rest of the night. I knew that was the safest place to be.

I stuffed myself with grass and grain thanks to the ranchers. Howard said they over-stuffed him with eggs and sausage as we headed out the next morning. Houses were non-existent on this new US 36. We rode into Hamilton for lunch where Howard stopped and chatted with three police officers. The more he talked the less I walked!

The easy day ended east of Cameron, behind a truck stop where the town had built a pavilion. I was put on a picket line, which allowed me to stay under the roof when it rained. Howard slept on one of the tables. That did not look too comfortable.

After no breakfast for me we rode in sunshine for the first time in nine days. The sunny, warm day was just gorgeous and the miles just eased on by. Howard found me oats for brunch, plus I always ate grass on the side of the road. Lunch for Howard meant he tied me up on concrete in Stewartsville but at least he did not stay too long.

Toward evening Howard turned off 36 onto a county road. The shoulders were lousy but I managed. A few miles later, we stopped at a barn where a couple and their teenage daughter came out to greet us.

"Good news Misty," Howard said as he stripped off my gear. "We are staying here for four days. That will give you a chance to have a good rest."

At the hitching post Howard gave me my first shower since forever it seemed. His strong hands and fingers massaged my aching muscles as he pushed the soap all over my coat. I even let him wash my face without much fuss.

As he led me into a one-acre paddock, another horse came into view. Howard let me go and the other horse decided that I was a problem. Approaching on my blind side, he kicked me hard. I bolted to the left and ran right through the single strand, electric fence.

"Misty, Misty," Howard cried out, "Stop!"

I did stop after going through the fence. I suffered a small cut but otherwise no harm. Bob came up, grabbed my enemy, and led him into another paddock.

I stood off to the side thinking, 'Can't we all get along here?'

After he and Howard fixed the fence, they brought in another, much older horse. He and I became friends. Howard and Bob watched nervously from the fence.

The next four days were wonderful. My only exercise was walking around the paddock to nibble on grass. Howard fed me grain four times a day and if I had lost a few pounds, I was back to full weight before we left. My barn buddy and I swapped a few stories, though he still could not imagine my journey. My detailed accounts of crossing the Ohio and Mississippi Rivers, sleeping behind billboards, tied to metal trashcans and the stories about how so many people had helped us made my pasture mate a believer.

I noticed Howard spent the days not moving much either. Evenings often meant an outdoor barbecue with several neighbors, prepared by Debbie and Emily. Howard told stories and the people liked to listen. Every few minutes he made them laugh at something.

The days of free-flowing grain and hay came to an end when Bob trailered us back to the main highway. A sunny, nice day greeted us as we headed into St. Joseph. The highway became a super highway and Howard decided to walk rather than ride in the heavy traffic. After about three miles, we came to the Missouri River again and Howard mounted up for the ride across the bridge. The bridge rose into the sky but not nearly as tall as in St. Louis. Three minutes on the bridge was all we needed to cross. A very large "WELCOME TO KANSAS" sign greeted us on the other side.

CHAPTER 6—JAYHAWKS AND PRAIRIE STATE

The flat, river flood plain made for easy going the first couple of miles. Howard was staking me out on the café sign in Wathena, when a couple of the waitresses stepped out to greet us. They rubbed and scratched me all over. Howard beamed like a new papa. He explained how we had already ridden almost half way across America.

After Howard walked me through town, we spent a pleasant, sunny afternoon riding to Troy. "Pony Express Highway" the sign proudly proclaimed as we left the small town of Wathena. Route 36 was the route taken by those mail carriers in the 1800's.

They named US 36 the Pony Express Highway and we saw a few signs showing a horse and rider. Although we were not in a hurry like they were, I imagined my equine brothers galloping across this road, carrying the mail 150 years ago. Their lives and mine were much the same and very different. They ran at a full gallop for hours and then had a few days off. I was traveling 25 miles a day but only one day off a week. I could imagine swapping stories with them. They had Indians, grizzlies and mountain lions on their tails and I have monster 18-wheeler Peterbilt trucks bearing down on mine.

The 22-mile day eased us back into the routine without overdoing it. We camped at a city park on the side of a hill where Howard let me graze. A good ole boy in a pickup gave Howard a soda and left me four flakes of hay. That night on the picket line, I sniffed the hay. It was foul. I nosed through the flakes trying to find something not too rotten but no luck. Howard noticed my predicament and quickly threw the flakes in the trash can.

"Sorry girl but that hay was only fit for cows," he lamented.

I passed a quiet night, recalling Howard's words that we were almost half way to the Pacific.

The new roadway featured good shoulders and we made fast time. Between the loping, munching and walking routine, the miles clicked off. One thing that I noticed was the "clink, clink, clink" of Howard's spurs as he paced off the miles. As he walked, my hooves beat a steady rhythm of "clop, clop, clop." It was an odd arrangement that a two legged human and a four legged horse made a kind of music along that lonely highway. At times, when the traffic roared past, I couldn't hear his spurs or my hooves beating out our movement westward. But when the traffic vanished, again the "clink, clink, clink" of Howard's spurs sang out in the early morning and the "clop, clop, clop" of my hooves became a steady assurance that we were making our way across this vast North

American continent. In front of us, we saw a vast grassy plain with barbed wire fences on each side of the highway. Black birds perched on fence posts. Every so often, a hawk dove out of the sky for a field mouse. Crows squawked their complaints at their friends. Men sitting on tractors plowed the land and always gave Howard a wave of their hands. The one constant was Howard's spurs and my horse shoes breaking the silence.

With the gathering twilight, his spurs and my hooves sang out at the growing thunderheads and the sun's scarlet rays spraying across the heavens in front of us. I couldn't help but feel a kindred sense of wonder with Howard. You see, I am a herd animal and Howard was my partner, and my friend. He depended on me and I depended on him. And so, into the thousands of miles, I felt assured as I heard the steady beat of his spurs going "clink, clink, clink" while my hooves plodded out the "clop, clop, clop" of a horse moving toward the Pacific Ocean.

After a late lunch in Hiawatha, Howard decided to keep riding all the way to the town of Fairview. It made for a hard 36-mile day, even though Howard walked 13 miles himself. At the west edge of town, he led me to a baseball field and its thick, lush grass. Howard busied himself with closing off a few gates, filling my water bucket and then walked to a café. Though I was content with dinner, I nickered loudly to him not to leave me. I don't like to be left alone.

"Okay," he shouted back. "I will make it a quick dinner and be back before dark." He promised. 'Sure,

sure', I thought. He starts 'politikin' and is gone for hours.

Only 90 minutes later and before dark, I spotted him from 200 yards away and screamed at him. Actually, I was happy to see him back so soon. He snuggled into his tent while I lay down near it to enjoy the comfort of his presence and companionship. Howard is a good cowboy. He learns from his mistakes. He changes to meet the demands of the day. He also likes to talk. It seems like the further we continue into this long ride, he has more stories for strangers.

Howard apologized as he saddled me near the pitcher's mound. "Hey, Misty," he said next morning. "I am sorry about yesterday. We'll do an easy 24 miles to Baileyville."

The rolling hills of Kansas made my life a lot easier. In Seneca, Howard found a corral for me while he ate lunch at a place called Fort Markley. An old cowboy named PJ stepped out to take a look at me and give me a lunch of sweet feed and hay. Next to me was his Arab horse, Jasmine. PJ had her do some tricks like "shake" rollover and play dead. While I respected Jasmine and her ability to do tricks, I was happy to be a Long Rider horse. I'm not in the same pasture everyday. I've met many equines along the road and they all want to hear my adventure stories. My confidence to handle any situation or hardship grows daily. Tested and retested, I am stronger and smarter than I was on the beach in Georgia. I dream of the day I meet another Long Rider horse and swap stories with him or her.

The sunny, warm day followed us into the small village of Baileyville. Howard and I went straight to the grain elevators. He came out with my feedbag and set it down for me to munch, while he chatted with the man. I stuck my nose into the bag and all I could find were oats. I started rooting around for sweet feed, tossing lots off oats that fell on the concrete.

"Misty!" Howard yelled. "What are you doing wasting those oats? You little stinker! The man gave us the oats for free and you are wasting them!"

Howard snatched the feedbag away and tried to put some of the oats back in the bag. He was funny that way. I watched him pick up any excess oats that I had missed as we traveled across the country and put them back into my feed bag. He knew they possessed precious nutrients to keep my body healthy.

Howard led me to a spot between the gas station and hair salon, and parked me on a picket line. He ate dinner across the street. Later that night he offered me the oats again and now realizing that was the only choice, I munched down.

An uneventful morning brought us into Marysville in the early afternoon after a 25-mile day. Howard parked me at the feed store on the east side of town, emerging with a 40-pound sack of sweet feed. He slung the sack onto the saddle and walked me about a mile to a park near the train tracks. As he began feeding me the first of the grain, he told me tomorrow was a rest day. 'Good', I thought and maybe he could find a shower because he smelled worse than the south end of a northbound mule.

As he wandered off in the direction of the library, I chewed my grain and noticed many squirrels running along the ground and through the trees. I later learned that Marysville is famous for its black squirrels. A long train whistled by and a few minutes later another, and then another. The tracks were only 100 feet from me and vibration and noise shook the ground.

A few hours later Howard returned clean-shaven and sniff, sniff, he smelled good, too. Thank you! He told me how Jackie, an 80-year-old woman, had just called off her porch to invite him in for coffee and cake. An hour later he departed that house all cleaned up. He went over me carefully as he did every few days.

"What is this Misty?" Howard asked.

He was touching my point of the hip where I was just beginning to develop a bald spot about twice the size of a horse's eye. It did not hurt but the hair was getting shorter and shorter. I could not tell him the solution. He would have to figure that out by himself.

The next day Howard led me around a bit, plus turned me loose to munch on grass all over the park. Howard said he visited the local Pony Express Comfort Station museum.

The warm sun and light breeze were countered by the incessant drone of the passing trains. Howard explained that Marysville is where the crews of the Union Pacific changed off and that is why the sound of the trains never stopped.

I felt good after a day off and combined with good shoulders, we covered 11 miles before lunch.

Howard fed me the last of the grain while he chowed down. We rode the next 11 miles into Washington. Howard found the fairgrounds to bed down for the night. Howard had switched the pads, which caused the thin spot to get worse in one day.

"Ooops, sorry girl," he apologized. "I'll try something else in the morning."

He left me in a mouse maze of an outdoor stall before he walked into town to eat. This time I did not yell at him, trusting him not to be tardy. He returned after an hour and bedded down just outside my stall.

I finished off the last of the grain at breakfast, which Howard had found the day before. I noticed Howard chatting with a cowboy during breakfast.

"Good news girl," he said. "We are spending the night 18 miles from here near Cuba. Nick has a working cattle ranch and we will be spending the night there."

The soft hills and flats of Kansas passed quickly. We rode up the driveway and bellowing bovines greeted us. Howard gave me a good shower before putting me in a stall surrounded by them. I watched him and Nick drive off in a big truck and trailer rig. The cattle made a racket all afternoon and it seemed half the night. I wanted to bite a few.

The next morning Howard and Nick took off again in the same rig. Finally, towards midday, we saddled up and rode off. The sharply rolling hills gave way to soft hills and flats. During his walk time, Howard explained what he and Nick had done. They had rounded up 37 head of cattle to deliver to a feedlot. Nick had used an ATV for the first time, instead of taking his trusty horse. Having my fellow equine replaced by a machine did not sit too well with me.

Around noon, a big 18-wheeler pulled in front of us and stopped. A large young man climbed out of the cab and approached us.

"Hey, my name is Tater and I've seen you two riding for weeks," he said. "What are you doing?"

"My name is Howard, my partner is Misty and we are riding across America," Howard replied.

"Dang! I thought you might be up to something crazy," he said. "Listen, I have a small house in Scandia and you are welcome to stay the night. Your horse could stay in the yard."

Howard accepted the offer and got directions. The 27 miles that day came and went and we loped into town toward Tater's house. Howard short-tied me to a tree, while he and Tater went out for dinner. Upon their return, a warm rain fell that continued all night.

The next morning Howard stopped at the post office and sent off a package. I suspected it was some unnecessary stuff because my cantle bag weighed two pounds less. Despite the rain, the shoulders were still in good shape and we made good time. Howard had lost two pounds and shifted some weight into the horn bags. The thin spot on my point of the hip improved from that day forward, until it disappeared.

The cloudy and mild 27-mile day went quickly, though towards evening we found ourselves in the middle of nowhere. Howard knocked on the door of Bob and Pat near Lebanon, asking them if we could use the barn across the street. Bob explained it was not his but we could stay at his place. Howard cleared a bunch of stuff away from two trees and hooked me up, before having his dinner in the house. Emerging a few hours later, he bunked down in the travel trailer next to me.

Howard made the next day an easy one, only traveling 28 miles to Kensington. The best part of the day occurred after breakfast. We passed a sign that said we were a few miles from the geographical center of the United States.

"Halfway done, girl," Howard sighed.

When we stopped at a café for lunch, a man came out and chatted with Howard.

"Nice looking' mare you got there," he said.

He went on to ask all kinds of questions about my heritage, our trip and me.

After Howard answered them all, he asked, "Is she for sale?"

I knew that Howard would say no and imagine my surprise when he replied, "Sure, she's for sale."

'WHAT?' I could not believe my ears. How could Howard be so nonchalant about selling me after all that we had been through?

"How much?" the man asked.

"$100,000.00," Howard responded.

"Cowboy, I am serious about buying your horse," he said. "She is a good-looking animal and I love her quiet disposition. She would be perfect for my nine-year-old daughter. Seriously, how much?"

With a calm voice Howard again said, "$100,000.00" and then added "cash, no check."

For a few seconds the man protested he was serious, finally realizing that I was priced not to sell. In the barns around the country, I had learned that most horses sell from between $500 and maybe $6,000.00. Howard had just been playing a little joke on the poor guy.

Howard camped at the city park, which featured a covered pavilion. Shortly after dark, the rain came pouring down. The wind was cool but Howard had strung the picket line behind a curtain of 15-foot shrub trees that blocked the wind well. Though I was soaked, I did not get cold.

The next day was an even shorter 15 miles into Phillipsburg. In the afternoon, my left front shoe became loose and Howard noticed it right away.

"We will have to find you a farrier tomorrow Misty," Howard said.

During the day, I noticed a sharp decrease in the amount of good grass on the roadside. During his one-mile walks, Howard allowed me to grab a mouthful of grass that I chewed while walking. When he sees me finished, he stops and we do it all over again. In this manner, I have been able to eat enough roughage to keep my system moving smoothly. I sure hope the grass situation does not get worse.

"Misty, you have been almost two days without grain and that is no good," Howard told me.

In the middle of the Phillipsburg, we took a right and headed for the grain elevator. Moments later, he threw a 50-pound bag on the saddle and we walked to the sub shop on Main Street. It was a concrete park job for me but Howard was only in there a few minutes. He exited with a sandwich and soda in hand. He led me about a half mile to a small corral and fed me a bunch of the equine senior feed. The night passed quietly and it was nice not to be on a picket line.

The morning started well with the farrier fixing my shoe and it was all down hill from there. The grass on the side of the road became all brown and worthless. It was hot and dry, although Howard found water. We traveled a hard 37 miles into Norton. Howard led me to the fairgrounds south of town and gave me a great shower. The water cascading on and down my body felt like heaven. There was no grass but luckily, there were lots of horses there for a clinic. The other horse owners sold Howard hay and grain.

We spent the next day there, resting and staying out of the hot sun. Howard sat in the grandstands while some trainers showed the riders how to communicate better with their horses. I could have told those riders all they needed to do was ride and sleep with their horse a couple of weeks straight. I could guarantee that communications would be much better.

The land flattened with sparse trees as we headed out after breakfast. There was no grass to eat during the day. We rode a half-mile off US 36 into Norcatur. Howard found lunch at the only café in town. A few minutes after he and a woman led me a few blocks to a barn. After Howard dumped off all my gear, we spent the rest of the day scouring the town for a bit of grass. We found enough to mostly fill me up but it was a struggle.

Howard picketed me on a wall of the barn and he slept in his tent on the other side. We departed out a little late because Howard ate breakfast with the family who owned the barn. The shoulders were good and the terrain continued flat to rolling hills. The fierce sun and cloudless sky created a hot and unrelenting misery. Another day passed without grass. Stopping for water at a farmhouse, Howard found no one home. We did find a working windmill that pumped water into a tank. I drank the cool, cool water deep and long. There were no towns until we arrived in Oberlin. Howard tied me up to the Pizza Hut sign and walked inside. I found a little grass to nibble on, as Howard took a long time to eat. A bunch of people stopped and came over to rub and scratch me. I felt like a celebrity. At the city park there was almost no grass and I went to sleep hungry.

I nickered at Howard the next morning as he crossed the street and headed for the café. He yelled back to be quiet and not wake the roosters. Ha ha! You're as funny as a mule, Howard.

The 29 miles to Atwood bored me to tears and it was a bit tough without a full stomach. Atwood had a feed store and Howard filled up the bag with oats. He walked me a bit further to a restaurant where he tied me to a parking meter. It was no fun to be left on concrete but at least I had all the oats I could eat. A reporter came up to say "Hi" to me, which caused Howard to leave his lunch and join us.

After the interview and meal, I was led back to the road and a park next to a lake. Howard led me around the park and I ate a decent amount of grass. An old cowboy came up and chatted with Howard a while. I was picketed between two huge trees and able to sleep soundly.

It was another 29-mile day of good shoulders and rolling hills. Does that sound boring? Every day was a challenge and required a great deal of physical energy and mental concentration. A 29-mile day means my hooves hit the ground about 41,000 times. Add to that my eye must focus every second on the shoulder ten feet ahead of us. Why? Because the roadsides are covered by bottles, cans, rocks, holes, wood with nails, re-rod, and whatever else people toss out windows or flies out the back of a pickup truck. Even with Howard also checking my steps, I break a glass bottle nearly every day. Howard always stops and checks my hoof for injury, to be safe. Each and every one of the 41,000 hoof falls could mean an injury or even a broken leg.

We made our way to the Bird City Park, which offered a tiny bit of grass. A local hippie came over and gave me two apples while he chatted with Howard. Though I normally don't like apples, I had learned not to refuse any food. Howard picketed me between two trees and we settled in for the night.

A few hours before dawn, the sky lit up with lightning and thunder a few miles north of us. Howard woke up and moved his stuff under a pavilion, expecting rain I guess. Howard started loading me up in the light of the park and walked me to a restaurant before daybreak. We left at first light.

The ride to St. Francis imitated the previous day, except a few miles outside of Bird City; a woman drove up and rolled down her window.

"I heard you were a retired cop riding across America," she said. "Is that true?"

"Yes ma'am. We are a little over half way across," Howard replied.

She handed Howard a large cup of coffee and a sack of doughnuts. He wolfed them down on the spot.

St. Francis had a nice park and a patch of grass that made me happy. Howard found some grain and I did not go to bed hungry. Howard enjoyed another shower and shave. It occurred to me that every town in Kansas had a free park for visitors. How thoughtful!

The town whistle blew at 7:00 AM sharp, making sure the whole town got up. I believe every little town in Kansas had this type of alarm clock and also the whistle would blow at 5:00 PM to tell people to stop working, I guess. Howard left me on the picket line while he had breakfast. 'Another hot day coming', I thought.

"Misty, today we will complete the state of Kansas and arrive in Colorado," Howard said. "That will mean we only have four states to go. But I must tell you they will prove the hardest of our ride."

I thought, 'At least that makes six states down and we are over half way'.

We headed out a bit late from Howard talking to town folks. Much of the day was flat and easygoing. We crossed the state line and trotted a few more miles to Idalia, Colorado before we camped for the night.

CHAPTER 7—COLORADO ROCKY MOUNTAIN HIGH

We spent the night a mile outside town where two highways joined up. The next morning Howard rode me into town and had breakfast at the local café. He spent longer than usual, which I did not mind, as there was some good grass in the café's yard.

After emerging from the eatery, he let me know what was going on.

"Misty," he said. "We are going to park it here for a day. We have been going at it pretty hard and we need a day off. Let's see if we can find you a bath."

A few minutes later, he tied me to the flagpole of the local post office. The postage stamp of a front yard provided some grass, while Howard received permission to use the water. Soon the cool water cascaded all over my body, as Howard worked the water into my coat and massaged my muscles. He gave me a 10-minute shower. I also knocked off several gallons of drinking water before we headed back. I passed the hot, lazy day in the shade of a few trees. Insects of all descriptions attacked me and my tail swished constantly, until Howard noticed.

"Misty, you poor thing," he said.

He sprayed me with human mosquito repellant.

"I had doubts about making you carry this extra six ounces of spray until now," he said. "I bet you are happy you did."

I cannot understand how there are so many of those little devils, when it is so dry.

The next morning Howard feasted at the same café. We walked over to the post office where Howard filled my water bucket again. A woman driving a pickup truck came by and that is when the fireworks started.

"Hey cowboy," she shouted in anger. "Yesterday, we only gave you permission to water your horse, not give her a bath."

"I am sorry ma'am," Howard said, meekly. "I didn't think it would be a problem to use a few more gallons of water. I'd be happy to pay the post office for the extra water."

"That is not the point," she said. "I want you to get your horse and leave town now."

"No problem ma'am and I am sorry for causing any trouble," Howard said. "We promise never to ride through Idalia again."

That lady rivaled the Wicked Witch of the North, but we had already passed through Kansas!

He led me down the sidewalk to US 36. After we reached the highway and the woman was long gone, Howard turned to me and said, "What do you think of that Misty? I reckon I was in the wrong but wow so much negative energy over a bath!"

I only remembered how great the shower felt. Like so many encounters good or bad on this journey, they were all soon in my rear view mirror. What counted was the road ahead. Doesn't make much horse sense for that lady to get upset over a few gallons of water for a weary horse and rider. If she were traveling through and needed help, she would appreciate a little neighborly care from local folks. Most Americans we've met on this ride have gone out of their way to help Howard and me. I wondered what burr she had under her life's saddle. Who rode her hard and put her up wet?

As the landscape became ever more barren of trees and grass, Howard made a short 17-mile day of it. Asking for water, he received permission to stay the night at a ranch east of Joes, Colorado. Howard led me to a large outdoor paddock and lots of hay and grain. Howard pitched his tent in the couple's backyard. It appeared he had dinner with them before easing into his tent.

The next morning we rode into the town of Joes for an early lunch. The highway was flat or gently rolling hills but there was a large increase in holes on the shoulder. Many were large enough to put my hoof into and it wore me out looking for them and the other debris on the side of the road. The relentless sun beat down on us, as the heat rose into the 90s.

Toward evening, Howard stopped me in the middle of nowhere. He stripped me and let me munch on a few scraps of grass near the ditch. Surely he wasn't planning on camping. There was not a tree or anything to tie me to, plus I was thirsty and hungry.

An hour or so before sundown I looked up to see a pickup truck slowing down and pulling off the road. As the tall, lean driver stepped out, I thought I was seeing Howard.

"Frosty, brother, great to see you," shouted Howard, as he came over and the two hugged.

"So this is Misty," the new man said.

He scratched under my ears and began to stroke my neck.

"Hi, girl. I'm Frosty, Howard's brother and guess what I brought you?"

With those words, he brought out several carrots, which I eagerly ate. Thus began a wonderful relationship with Frosty who always brought me carrots.

Frosty parked the truck, brought out grain, hay and water that I feasted on. Howard and Frosty built a small fire, before they ate their dinner. There was much conversation as the two laughed and talked for hours. Howard looped my reins over a nearby fence post and there I was parked for the night.

The next morning after a wonderful breakfast Frosty drove off as Howard walked me the usual quarter mile to warm me up. The sun broke on our backs as we loped off. It was a grinding, hot day full of insects, which the mosquito spray was only partially successful in keeping them in check. We pushed hard all day. Though I was able to drink as much as

I needed, the sun and heat punished me with every hoof fall of the 27 miles.

We arrived at a tiny little café in the village of Last Chance in the late afternoon. Howard parked me under a tree and went inside for a late lunch. Two hours later, Frosty arrived with more carrots and great food. I could get used to this luxury of having a great dinner and breakfast. Naturally, this situation would only last a few more days.

We got moving at the crack of daylight as Howard sought to avoid the heat of the day. The shoulder became almost non-existent for a stretch and Howard had me follow the ditch. I was loping along, when Howard and I both missed a gopher hole. My front left leg went down into the ground, throwing Howard forward. My nose and knee smashed into the ground as I completely lost my balance. I could feel Howard striving to shift his weight to the rear as I struggled to regain my balance. After another stride, I regained it and came to a stop, trembling. Howard leaped off to inspect the damage.

"How are you girl? Did you break anything? Let me see you walk."

He led me forward a few yards. Fortunately, I had not broken or even strained anything. I had a good scrape on my nose and knee, both of which showed blood but were not bleeding. I had been lucky.

Howard was able to find me water once that day. Luckily, I was in tremendous physical and mental condition and the lack of water was not a problem-- just a bit of discomfort. The trackless brown and gray landscape grew dreary and the sun pounded into me all day. I plodded to the end of the Great Plains like many of my ancestors. The 28 miles ended in between two towns and again Frosty showed up with dinner and treats. That evening, a dinner feast made the situation tolerable.

After breakfast the next day at a café in Byers, we walked under the expressway and through town. Dodging more trash on the side of the road, I figured we must be nearing a bigger city. I noticed a strange looking bank of clouds far on the western horizon after we left Byers. As the miles past, the clouds kept their position and seemed to change a bit. A few miles from Watkins, my mind was staggered by a clear view of the 'clouds'. Beneath the clouds were huge, snow-capped mountains and my heart sank and my mind reeled with the mere thought of having to go over them. On one of his walks, Howard stopped and we both looked upon the awesome grandeur, beauty and for us the challenge of those mountains.

"Those are the Rocky Mountains girl," Howard stated. "We will have to go over two passes at about 12,000 feet and they will be tough days. We will rest up before tackling them. I promise."

Toward evening, we rode into a truck stop in Watkins and camped for the night. The constant engine noise of the trucks reminded us of being close to a big city. After a while, I became used to the noise and drifted off. The engines were not any worse than the tugboats on the Ohio River.

Howard awoke before light and disappeared into the restaurant with Frosty who showed up late last night. At first light, we left the truck stop and were able to run about 10 miles before we encountered too much concrete and city. Denver's skyscrapers rose majestically into the sky and we headed right for them. Howard had to lead me most of the day, usually on sidewalks. Around noon, I started seeing these men with little signs in their hands. They looked pretty scruffy and a couple of times I was so close I could smell them. They were worse than Howard after a week of no showers. The little signs asked for money and sometimes people would stop their cars and hand them a dollar or something.

We were approaching the tall buildings when Howard stopped me at an outdoor café. Howard stripped off my gear and sat down at a table. I had to stay on the other side of a single strand of chain.

"What will you have, sir?" the woman asked Howard.

"Whiskey for me and a beer for my horse," he ordered.

"Are you serious?" she asked.

"Yes, it has been a long, hot day for both of us," he responded.

After a few minutes, she returned with the manager.

"How old is your horse?" the manager asked.

"Twenty-seven in human years," replied Howard.

"I can't serve your horse beer if he stays on the other side of the chain," the man said.

"Oh all right, I'll take the cold ice tea and a turkey sandwich and how about a bucket of water for Misty?"

"That we can get for you and everything is on the house," the manager said as both he and the waitress broke into big grins.

After lunch, Howard led me around several of the giant buildings, stopping at a structure with a dome on top. We walked on concrete sidewalks for the entire afternoon. My joints squealed and the constant sight of snow-capped mountains did not improve my spirits either.

The asphalt jungle finally ended when I stepped on grass near Golden. At that point, I was eyeball to eyeball with the mountains. Serious mountain terrain awaited.

A few miles later Howard tied me up next to a bunch of shiny, huge motorcycles. The sign read: "HARLEY DAVIDSON PARKING ONLY." The owner of the bar came out and asked Howard what was going on. Learning of our cross-country adventure, she made me an honorary Milwaukee Iron Horse and I was able to stand next to the bikes.

From my vantage point, I saw the snow-capped mountains in the distance and the road going straight up. It had been an exhausting day and I hoped Howard was thinking of a day off, before dueling with the mountains. My prayers were answered as I saw his brother Frosty drive up, not just with the truck but also with my horse trailer.

"Remember I promised you some time off, girl?" Howard inquired. "We are taking a whole week off. Both of us need to recharge our batteries."

'YES!' I relished the thought of a whole week off with Frosty giving me carrots every day! You've heard of pig heaven haven't you? Well, there's a horse heaven, too! It's one filled with green pastures knee deep in clover. A cool stream flows through one corner and three times a day, someone steps into the meadow with a bucket of carrots. Top it off with a half dozen of my girlfriends to run with and THAT'S horse heaven!

I hopped into the trailer and a few minutes later, I was out in my own paddock on a small ranch. This ranch I called home for the next week.

The week of rest charged up my batteries after going 600 miles without more than a day off. Howard only rode me a few minutes a day bareback, I had all the food I could eat and Frosty kept me supplied in carrots. What a life! The only black cloud in this picture occurred when I looked to the west and gazed on the snow-capped peaks. The highest mountain back east only took four hours to go up and down. These monsters would have to be all-day efforts. I knew Howard and I could do it but I was not looking forward to the challenge.

My pampered life ended. I heard Howard's spurs jangle when he walked up before daybreak to feed me. That sound meant we were on our way.

"Okay, this will be medium tough day," Howard said. "We will have a four-mile climb to the first pass and then down the other side. I know you will signal me, if you need to rest."

I guessed the mountains weighed heavy on his mind also.

After Frosty trailered us back to US 40, I overheard them say good-bye to each other and Frosty wished us luck.

"Misty, that was the last long break of the trip," Howard said. "We have about 1,400 miles and three months to go. However, they will be the hardest. There is precious little water, food or ranches ahead of us. We can do this and you know your health comes first."

His words fell heavily on my ears, as their meaning was clear. From the Atlantic to Denver had been the 'easy' half of the trip. All the trials and mistakes and hardships had simply been a preparation for the last four states. The bond Howard and I had formed was as solid as the Rockies. Confidence to go anywhere, do anything, well, I had it in hooves! It had been forged in the fires of the first 1800 miles.

Glancing down, I saw he was carrying a six-shooter on his hip. I wondered why he was carrying a weapon. The answer to that question came later in the day. Howard breathed slowly and deeply, as he stuck one foot in the stirrup and swung into the saddle. As he adjusted his seat, his heavy words swam in my brain. The last three months had been no picnic. Now the road would be harder. Aside from the mountains, every day would be more of a struggle. I set my mind on a tight focus and resolved to take one day at a time and let Howard worry about the big picture. I knew he trusted me and so, I trusted him.

Howard nudged me slightly with his ankle and I leaped forward at a hard lope. Though it was constant four-mile upgrade, my energy was tremendous from the time off and my body felt in superb condition. Besides, I love to run and Howard's yelling a few times put me in a good mood. Blowing hard after two miles, Howard reined me in and hopped off to walk his mile. I began to see all sized rocks on our path and I concentrated on missing them. Though the vistas were magnificent, I kept my gaze focused just a few feet ahead of me.

"Keep sharp girl," Howard said. "We've got rocks on the road and rocks could fall on our heads."

'WHAT?' Rocks on my head? What's up with that?

I dodged rocks for several miles that day. Later Howard told me it had not been his first experience with rocks. Years earlier he had ridden horses around the pyramids of Egypt and out into the desert. The desert sand was full of rocks and the quick Arabian horse he rode had also missed all of them.

After we crested the first pass, a car driven by a woman with her daughter who had seen us on TV, stopped to say "Hi" and wish us well. US 40 ceased to exist and we were forced onto a few miles of Interstate 70. This was a new experience for me, as the traffic was much heavier than the two lane roads. However, it was no big deal and a few minutes later, we turned back on a winding road. At the bottom of that hill was another café whose parking lot was full of motorcycles. The patrons of Kermit's Café let me park next to all the shiny Harleys again. The cook came out with a pair of huge carrots that I wolfed down. A table of bikers in black leather invited Howard over for lunch.

Leaving Kermit's, Howard led me down to a river and what appeared to be a bicycle path.

"Good thing Kermit's was there girl," Howard said. "US 40 ends and the expressway has a good-sized tunnel that would be dangerous. We are going to use this path that should lead us into Idaho Springs."

A fast-moving stream held kayakers and their brightly colored boats. I enjoyed the break from vehicle traffic for the mile or two the path lasted.

Howard led me through the city and out into the canyon behind. I felt edgy about this new terrain. 'Mountain lions could be living in this area', I thought. Though I had never seen one, my instincts told me this was a dangerous place. I hoped Howard was also aware of this new threat. Howard led me to a horse ranch and I was able to chew on a large portion of grain. The small rancher did not offer to let us spend the night and reluctantly we left. It would have been a comfort for me to be near their four horses.

A few minutes later Howard stopped for the night near the road and a business. Using the canvas bucket, he fetched me water from the river. After munching on all the grass he could find me, he hooked me up to the picket line. I had a good view of the rocky crags above me. Pine trees grew out of solid rocks. Aspen grew along the rivers and in patches high above us. In a situation like this, a single horse has to sleep with one eye open, but, horse-hooves, I only had one eye. After Howard went to sleep, I stayed awake most of the night--fearful of an attack. Luckily, I never saw any animals and toward dawn, I caught an hour of sleep. Knowing that Howard had the pistol comforted me. Back in Texas, he had acclimated me to the great noise it made. That alone would scare off a cougar.

Right after taking off the next morning, we passed a corral. I wish we could have camped there last night! I dislike being on a confining picket line. Howard parked me on the street in the town of Empire for a late breakfast. Again, the cook brought me some carrots while I waited on the asphalt for Howard to finish. I must have been quite a tourist attraction as a half-dozen people came up to pet me.

As we left the small town, I noted the new weight in the horn bags. Howard carried his own water for the first time since Georgia. It was only a few pounds and he had dropped the weight in the cantle bag to only 12 pounds. The gun became part of Howard's live weight, so its burden was slight. The mental comfort of knowing Howard could kill a cougar or wild dog made the additional work a minor detail.

The highway maintained a steady incline for the next few miles. Tall pines grew on mountainsides everywhere I looked. Canyons fell away from us while tall mountain peaks brushed against the sky. Looking up, I saw the cuts in the mountain and tiny cars miles over my head. I realized that was where we were going and it depressed me. Thin air made breathing a problem. Progressing past a few cabins on the left, I had to break out of my lope and into a trot. Howard sensed my distress and after only a mile on my back, he dismounted and led me the next mile.

"Bad timing on me carrying my own water girl," Howard said. "Sorry."

He said we had entered the 'no spit zone' of America and for the next thousand miles, water would be a precious resource.

"I have to drink enough water or else I won't be able to walk my ten miles per day," Howard explained.

Making a hard right curve the road climbed steeply. Howard mounted up and I loped only a few strides before slowing to a trot and then to a walk. My lungs protested as my breathing increased. Bless Howard for noticing my struggle. Though we had only gone 200 yards, he hopped off and led me. I noticed his breathing had also become shallow and rapid.

Torture explains the next few hours as we made our way up the pass. We stopped often to catch our breath. When he rode me, I only could manage a walk. Even trotting was out of the question. The sun went behind a bank of clouds and the air cooled quickly. The only good news was the layer of sand that covered the asphalt in many places. It did soften the pounding my hooves were taking because the route had almost no soft shoulders. The muscles in my legs ached from the constant strain of pushing me up that mountain. My lungs screamed in protest as they moved the thin air in and out, seemingly without taking in any oxygen.

Finally, the steep incline became flat and I was grateful. This mountain however had no intention of letting me off. It began to sleet hard and the freezing rain hit my exposed flanks, neck and eye. Howard stopped immediately and pulled his rain jacket out of the cantle bag. But instead of putting it on, he put it over my head, protecting my eye. Bless him! It would not be the last time he had to protect my eye.

After a few minutes, the sleet storm moved off and we rode past the sign "BERTHOUD PASS Elevation 11,161 feet." Moments later, we descended. The downhill did not seem as steep as the uphill climb but it was still hard on my leg joints. The saddle pushed into my withers with every stride and I had already learned what damage that could do to my thin skin. Howard knew it too, as he leaned back in the saddle to lessen the pressure of the saddletree on the sensitive spot. After only a mile, he stepped down and we continued this one-on, one-off all the way to the valley floor.

Howard remained true to the code of the Long Rider; take care of the horse first.

A sea of green trees greeted my eye as we neared the bottom. OUCH! My left hip muscle barked in protest and I dipped down in response to the pain. A minute later, I felt the same sharp jab of pain and dipped down again.

"Darn girl! You are not all right, are you?" Howard said.

I looked back at him and let my ears do the communicating for me. Howard read the cues and dismounted.

"I'll walk the rest of the way into town girl. You just went over an 11,000-foot pass and we still have five miles to go. I don't want you to hurt yourself. I am not sure how much pain you have or what damage has been done but I know I can walk into town if you can."

The walk into Winter Park proved a long one. Howard was dog-tired and his pace slowed, punctuated by many breaks. He showed haggard eyes plus he limped. He was beat but he still did not take the easy way out by riding me. The dark skies became black as daylight faded. The "Welcome to Winter Park" sign came into view just as the skies opened up and a cold rain pummeled us. Could this day get any worse? We walked off the road toward a barn but Howard could not find anyone so we went back to the roadway. Drenched to the bone, we were passing the first motel when a man came out and greeted us.

"What in the world are you doing?" he asked Howard.

"Riding across America," Howard replied.

"Holy smokes," he said. "I can see your horse needs shelter badly and you don't look so good yourself. My name is Craig and let's find a stall for your horse."

A second later, his nine-year-old daughter, Jessica, came out into the pouring rain to help lead us back to the barn we had just passed. Craig led us to a tiny stall near the main barn. Howard coaxed me into the 8 X 4-foot box. Using the lariat, he fashioned a web across the entrance so I could not get out. Meanwhile Craig and Jessica scrounged around the barn and were able to find me some hay. I was so thankful to be out of the cold rain and wind that the meager dinner was not a problem. The main area of my back had stayed dry because of the saddle.

Earlier I described what horse heaven would look like. Today had been a horse nightmare. Yet, even as my muscles and joints kept screaming in pain from going over the pass, I felt a sense of elation, as if I had won a race or received the blue ribbon. My mom and dad would be proud of me and beam--when they learned what their daughter had done this day. While such thoughts danced in my head, I fell asleep.

Bright and early the next morning Howard came down and found more hay. After disappearing for an hour, he returned with grain that he fed me in a small paddock that had a small brook running through it. The sunshine had returned and the temperature climbed fast.

"We are taking a rest day here girl," Howard said. "The mountain kicked both of us in."

Shortly after breakfast, I relaxed in the green grass and let the warm sun cover my still-aching body. We had covered 50 miles in the past two days and I needed the rest.

The next morning Howard started my day off with more hay. Loaded up, Howard led me to a local café for his breakfast where I ate my grain. Leaving town, he simply told me to go at whatever speed I felt comfortable. I loped off for two miles, feeling okay. Howard stopped me at the big grocery outside of Fraser and tied me to a light pole. He came out with six carrots, which he let me eat on the spot. As I enjoyed the taste treat, a local guy drove up in a pickup. He chatted with Howard for a few minutes, giving us two short cuts to the next town of Granby.

West of Fraser, Howard had me leave US 40 and move onto a county road. I loped off at a good pace feeling good about saving some miles, when UGGHH my right, front leg went down to the knee in a soft patch of dirt. Howard was flung forward, compounding my balance problem as my nose smashed into the dirt. Howard struggled to lean backwards and after another step, I was able to regain my stride. Howard quickly stopped me and hopped off.

"Oh man Misty. Are you okay? Your nose is a mess and how is your leg?"

He touched the back of my ankle and I lifted up my leg. He touched all the joints, feeling for a pulled tendon or worse. I knew I was okay, just shaken up and a minute later Howard, too, was satisfied that no serious injury had occurred. Twice in Colorado I had stumbled and twice the damage was slight.

The sunny, mild day made the going pleasant and Howard even found a soft horse trail, which kept us off the roadway. After an hour or so, he slowed me to a walk and then asked a worker, if this path led to Granby. Howard thanked the man and dismounted.

"Sorry Misty," Howard said. "That guy in Fraser gave me bad advice and we have to turn around."

It was a four-mile mistake, which put us into Granby late in the afternoon. Howard found me a bit of sand to stand on while he ate at the Silver Spur Saloon. Emerging, he was smiling.

"Got half off the dinner because I had my spurs on Misty," he said.

Just west of town, he led me onto a horse ranch. The owner met us halfway down the driveway. The rancher said we could not stay because I might be carrying diseases. Howard showed the man my health papers but it didn't matter and we loped off into the gathering darkness. A mile later Howard led me to a barn near the river. Howard looked for someone to ask and finding none, roped me off into a 30 X 30 area, which contained a stack of hay bales. What is that? I riveted my attention to two figures about 100 yards away on the riverbank. I wanted to run away but Howard was holding me tightly.

"Misty, those are two deer, not cougars," Howard explained.

I still wasn't sure and for 20 minutes I eyed those beasts, until they ran off.

Dinner included hay and water but no grain. Howard pitched his tent in my makeshift paddock and climbed in. Howard had opened a bale, after he put four dollars on one of the bales and I did have plenty. After a few hours though, I became curious if one of the other bales might have better hay. I began to paw at it with my front, right hoof. The bale's metal wire became stuck between my hoof and shoe, just as I was successful in breaking the bale open.

"Misty, you okay?" Howard's voice pierced the darkness.

I nickered to him to let him know I had a problem. Wearing his miner's light on his forehead, he emerged with his gun in one hand and his multi-purpose tool in the other. He quickly diagnosed the problem and put his gun down. He calmed me down, had me lift my hoof and then used the tool to extract the wire.

"Misty! You had plenty of hay but you just had to open another bale. Please don't do it again."

Shortly after my curiosity landed me in trouble, I fell asleep.

Packing up early, Howard was startled by the barn owner showing up. Randy said he had no problem with us being there overnight and we were welcome to the hay. An hour later Howard stopped in Hot Sulphur Springs at the café. He found a bit of grass for me. As usual, Howard came out the door of the café every five minutes or so to check on me. After about 20 minutes, he discovered I had stepped on the rein and broken it. He reattached me to the speed limit sign and went back inside to finish his breakfast. It took him the usual 10 minutes to fix the reins. He used to scold me for breaking the reins but I guess he is now used to it.

A few miles later Howard stopped at a ranch for grain. No one was home but he went into the barn and came out with enough for one meal. I was grateful for the calories. An elderly woman came home while I was eating. Howard went over and explained how he had left some money for the grain. She told him to keep the money but did ask when we were leaving.

"Right after my horse finishes eating," he replied, looking puzzled by the question.

She was satisfied with that answer and went inside.

I was amazed at the differences in human beings. Some were trusting while others were wary. Some seemed happy while others seemed unhappy. Some made a big deal out of nothing while others made nothing out of their generosity. Others wanted to ride with us while still others thought we were crazy for riding coast-to-coast. All of them brought a different emotional response to Howard and me. I wondered what made them act so differently.

We wound our way through Byer's Canyon. Sheer rock cliffs jutted up from the road into a brilliant blue sky with a river bursting into whitewater far below us. Along the river, a train wound its way through the canyon. The conductor waved to Howard who tipped his cowboy hat. Above us, hawks soared along the craggy cliffs. This sure beat the scenery in Kansas.

In the small town of Kremmling, Howard led me to the fairgrounds where he found an uncovered stall. A man in a pickup had followed us and Howard left with him. A few minutes later, they returned with hay and grain and I was soon stuffed. Even better, Howard gave me a long shower with his usual massaging as he sprayed me. Then I was left alone, except for Howard feeding me again at dusk.

At dawn the next morning, we rose with the sun for an early start.

"Good news Misty," Howard said. "Richard has a rancher friend 25 miles up the road and we are all set to spend the night there. That is doubly good because the next town is 52 miles away."

I loped off in a good mood with such news. The landscape had changed severely and there was not a blade of grass to be eaten.

The first miles out of town proved easy with roller coaster hills. However, by mid-morning the steady shoulders became spotty with trenches to avoid. The road climbed a slow, steady up and air became ever thinner as I struggled toward Rabbit Ears Pass.

Past midday, Howard directed me off US 40 and down toward some houses and barns on the west side of the road. A few minutes later, a man came out of the log home and drove to us. This must be the ranch Howard had mentioned earlier. The two men chatted for a few moments and the man drove off up into the hills. Howard's dejected face told the story as he informed me that we had no place to stay for the night.

Howard tied me to a hay wagon and got me some water, so at least I had a good lunch.

After double-checking how securely I was attached, Howard drove off with a young man. They had been gone only a few minutes, when I heard bellowing of many bovines. A few minutes later, I saw a herd of 200 cows and calves being pushed and guided by five cowboys on horseback. I smelled the burnt hide on the sides of the calves and saw their fresh brand marks. It was quite a sight for this city-oriented horse.

After about an hour, Howard returned.

"It is not good Misty," Howard said. "The place the owner's son showed me is too far off the road to go to. We will just have to keep moving and hope we find something. Sorry girl."

The rancher's wife arrived about that time and Howard was able to eat a sandwich and make one for dinner. Looking lower than a well digger's boot, Howard led me back to the road.

We continued the steady climb up the valley for another hour before we came to a place near the road with horses. Howard knocked long and hard on the house door but no one was home. I munched on the grass in the yard while Howard just stretched out and rested nearby. Howard was unable to find any water but it had only been a few hours. Toward dusk, Howard ate his sandwich and took a few sips from his water bottle.

He put me in a round pen next to a paddock with two fat horses. Howard snagged some hay out of their manger and gave it to me. The fat horses snorted and expressed their displeasure but Howard paid them no mind.

Howard pitched his tiny tent just outside the round pen and climbed inside. A few minutes later the whole valley echoed with howling coyotes. There had to be dozens of them up in the hills across the highway. First a few and then more cows with the calves came streaming out of the hills and down toward to the safety of the center of the valley. About 400 bunched up in the pasture. The howling was incessant for an hour. They sounded so close, I was sure they were only yards away. Howard poked his head out of the tent and then came out to investigate.

"I don't think they are too close Misty and they would go after the calves before you or me," Howard said. "Still I will sleep with my gun close. You scream if you see one."

Though I was tired from the constant climbing, I remained on full alert for several hours. Around midnight one of the fat horses turned to me, "Hey Paint. Those coyotes are not going to bother us. Go to sleep and I will stand guard."

"Thanks pal," I answered. "I appreciate you letting me sleep. Sorry about my partner taking your hay."

"No sweat Paint," the stallion nickered. "Our master will give us plenty more in the morning."

Howard crawled out of the tent at first light and we hit the road early. While breaking camp, I saw Howard eat his candy bars for breakfast. Walking down the driveway, he gave me a preview of the day.

"Misty today we are going to cross Rabbit Ears pass at over 12,000 feet," Howard said. "It will be as bad as the one last week west of Denver. I should be able to find you water but I am nearly out and I can't drink out of a lake or stream. Besides water, I have no food and there is no café until town. We will be successful and tonight we will camp in Steamboat Springs. It will be a hard 27-mile day and I wanted you to prepare for it mentally. I will ride you as little as possible but without food in my stomach, I may have to ask more from you. It is definitely a 'cowboy up' kind of a day."

After only a few minutes, I saw the rock formation for which the pass was named. The shoulders improved as we reached the switchbacks. Massive reconstruction on the roadway made us wait for big trucks and scrapers. Howard found a lake where I had a long drink. Howard spotted a camper and I was happy for him that the couple was able to let Howard drink and leave him a quart bottle. I think he was too proud to ask for food.

Before midday, the switchbacks stopped and we entered a 10-mile long plateau area. Even with the altitude I was mostly able to maintain a lope in the cadence of run two, be led one-mile routine. I was not just in the best physical condition of my life, I felt I could do anything Howard asked and my body would respond. My muscles rippled and carried us over those 10 miles in no time.

As we began our descent, Howard walked. Perhaps the failure of Georgia still haunted him when he rode me down the hills that caused my injuries.

A beautiful valley opened up below us as we made our steady progress. Howard ran out of water halfway down and he began limping about the same time. Still, he refused to hop on my back.

At mid-afternoon, we reached the bottom and Howard hopped on to ride. Less than a mile later, we stopped at a large horse ranch and I munched a generous helping of grain. Howard looked terrible. His drawn face and tired eyes showed him without energy and he could only lay next me--as I tore into the grain. Rising slowly, he mounted up again and we rode into Steamboat Springs toward evening. For one of the few times of the ride, he was limp in the saddle with shoulders stooped.

About the city limits, Howard dismounted and led me a good two miles through town. He spotted his favorite Pizza Hut on the right side and led me over. Tying me to a tree with some grass around it, he slowly took off my gear. He left and came back with a large bucket of water, which I needed. He refilled it before he limped into the restaurant. I just hoped his injury was temporary and he was okay. I had no injuries and knew I was healthy.

After an hour, Howard emerged looking better. He even smiled for the first time that day. He led me across the street to a soccer field and turned me loose on the grass. Ever the cowboy, he walked behind me and removed my poop with his gloved hands. Later he led me down to the river to drink and eat more grass.

At dark, he strung his lariat on the soccer goal posts and hooked me up. I had a good, clear view and felt confident sleeping with him nearby. I was sleeping soundly, when a heavy stream of water hit my body. AAHHHH! I was so startled that I pulled back hard on the goal post, pulling it over and breaking the rein to boot. Howard heard the commotion and got out of his tent. The cold water splattered all over him.

"What the heck?" he screamed.

At the same time, we realized that the automatic sprinklers had come on at midnight. Howard put the goal back in place and tied a knot on the rein to fix it for the rest of the night. His tent was waterproof so he climbed back in after securing me. The periodic shower I got for the next hour felt pretty good after the hard, hot last two days on the road.

The next morning Howard fixed the rein and walked me to a café in the middle of what I guessed was an older part of town. He hooked me up to a light pole at a café with outside tables. Many patrons came up and petted me as if I was some kind of big dog. They would "uuh and ahhh" and if I had a flake of hay for every time I heard the words 'poor thing' in relation to my eye, I'd be a fat horse. Oh well. It is a horse's life. As I whinnied about the morning, the server came outside and fed me two carrots. 'Unexpected kindness is always the best', I thought.

Howard stopped by the post office and I saw him take in a small package. Returning he explained.

"I just mailed my rain gear, sweater and sleeping bag to Vale, Oregon girl," Howard said. "I have kept the mummy bag and if it gets cold, I'll use the horse blankets. It will save you about four pounds. We are about to enter the 'land of not much'. We are heading into a thousand miles of pure desert. The sun and heat will be worse. There will be no grass and no running water. I will make sure you are fed. We are now both in world-class shape both physically and mentally. We can do it."

I sighed heavily at this news. Yes, we could and would do it.

"I should be able to get you some grain at this vet's office Misty girl," Howard said as he hopped off and tied me to a tree.

I stood at the west edge of town and after 48 hours and one mountain pass with no grain, I wanted real food. Seeing the disgusted look on his face informed me that Howard had not been successful.

"I can't believe it girl," Howard said. "I offered to buy two scoops and it was a no go. I sure hope the rest of the trip won't be like the last two days, for your sake and mine."

Howard hopped on at the edge of town and I did start out at a lope but I could only hold it a mile. I felt tired from the previous day. The rest of the day, I trotted my two miles instead of a lope.

Around midday, we arrived at a ranch with lots of people and cars and things for sale. In a large paddock at the center of the activities were four mares and their young foals. More importantly, Howard provided me a huge portion of grain most of which I ate. He put the rest in the grain bag and I carried it the remainder of the day. I know Howard did not like me carrying grain but ranches were becoming scarcer with every passing day.

After 25 miles, Howard led me to what had to be a place to camp next to the river. After 45 minutes of fruitless searching, he gave up and led me back to the road. Two miles later, we stopped. Howard turned me loose to chew the sparse, brown grass. It was barely better than nothing. Howard strung the lariat up on the ground-level billboard and hooked me up for the night.

It only took us an hour to reach the town of Hayden and park at The Main Street café. It was another hard park for me on the concrete but at least the cook came out with a bunch of carrots. A teenager helped Howard by fetching me a large bucket of water. A few miles out of town, Howard and I spotted a horse ranch and we pulled in. After Howard tied me to a fence and disappeared with the rancher, a gorgeous black stallion came over to the edge of his paddock and said "Hello."

'Oh my', I thought. I would want you to be the daddy to my children but now is not the right time. I ate a nice brunch of oats and hay, and I was happy to see Howard take some with him.

We passed a number of ranches but they all had cattle guards and many had fences across their entrances, making it impossible to ask for water. After midday, Howard led me into a rest area, hoping to find me water. Howard stopped near a woman and asked if there was water to drink.

"Only Germany," she replied. "Only Germany."

"Kein problem," Howard responded. "Wissen Sie ob es hier Trinkwasser gaebe?"

The sounds Howard made had no meaning to me. I was a strictly English understanding horse. The woman responded with something and pointed to her husband. He and Howard continued in this strange language for 10 minutes before we left…without any water unfortunately.

A few miles later Howard was feeding me the last of the grain, when a couple drove up and came out with a TV camera. Howard was still so tired he did not even get up to shake hands and the man interviewed him by squatting.

On the east edge of Craig, Howard stopped at a house with horses. After a brief conversation, he emerged from the barn with my feed bag bulging with grain. 'Good', I thought. Tonight I sleep with a full stomach. A few minutes later, we did something very unusual; we stopped at a real campground. Howard wanted a shower and a no hassle night of camping. I knew we were on a tight budget, so it came as a surprise. After stripping off my gear, he led me back to the office and gave me a most-welcomed shower. After days in the boiling sun, heat and the hard work, the shower felt wonderful. After the massage, Howard kept the water pouring all over me.

We scrounged the campsite for grass for two hours before Howard hooked me up to a picket line. He put the grain bag in front of me and I dove in. Yuk! What is this? Birdseed? After one bite, I tried to find some grass.

"Is it that bad girl?" Howard asked.

My response was to knock the bag over and try to find some grass underneath. "I know it looks weird girl but the ranchers' horses eat it. Please try to eat it tonight," he pleaded.

Later a car drove up and delivered a large pizza. The massive amount of food vanished in short order. With a large burp and belch, Howard walked over to the shower room and cleaned up. I felt secure enough to lie down to sleep that night. Later that night, I ate the grain. By daybreak I was back to 100 percent.

We walked the mile into Craig and once again, Howard had to tie me to a light pole on concrete to eat breakfast. On the west edge of town, he stopped at the big grocery store, returning with lots of carrots, and feeding me half of them. A few miles out of town, a couple in a van stopped us. They offered a gallon of water and Howard drank his fill. He still carried only one quart of water.

A few miles later Howard found a ranch without a cattle guard and we trotted up. I enjoyed oats and fly spray. For the first time in a month, the bugs attacked again. The woman used a cloth to cover my body and it was nice not to be tormented. Howard filled the fly spray bottle before we left.

The merciless sun was coupled with not a tree anywhere. By mid-afternoon, I was ready for more water and luckily, Howard found a house. No one was home but Howard took me in the backyard anyway. Howard filled my bucket with water several times before I was satisfied. Howard propped himself in the shade against the wall of the house, while I munched down on the lush grass of the backyard.

"This is the only shade in 30 miles girl," Howard informed me.

A few miles outside of Maybell, Todd Weber filled up my grain bag from which I ate while he and Howard chatted.

"You and the horse look like you need some rest," he told Howard.

"You would be right about that," Howard replied. "It has been a very tough week and 160 miles."

"There is a corral north of town that you could stay at," the man said. "I'll drop off some hay for the horse, enough for a full day of rest."

"Much obliged mister," Howard said. "This is hard livin' making 25 miles a day in this heat."

At the Maybell café, Howard got me water and then a shower before he went inside to eat. After a 32-mile day, I was pooped. Howard rode me at a walk to the corral. Mr. Weber had dropped off a

100-pound bale. I could never eat it but I would try. Howard gave me 20 pounds to chew for the night. A man from across the street helped make sure all the gates were closed before turning me loose.

"You want an ice cold soda, cowboy?" the man inquired.

"You giving me a soda pop today will guarantee you going to heaven, sir," Howard responded. They both laughed and left me for about an hour.

Howard set up his tent inside the arena and fell asleep. A few coyotes howled as the moon rose over the low hills. I moved close to Howard's tent and felt safer. Soon, I too, fell asleep.

Another cloudless day broke over Colorado's eastern sky. I mentally prepared for a grueling day. I thought how strange it was that Howard did not start taking down his tent. Then he hopped on my bareback and we began walking toward town. Only then did I remember that today was a rest day and Howard must be headed back to the café. Thank you!

Returning to the corral after breakfast, Howard left me alone with lots of hay and water. He told me he would be spending the day at the village library reading a book on how to ride a horse. He laughed at his own joke as he walked back into town. Made me wonder what makes humans tick.

Up early to beat the heat, we left the Maybell café at daybreak. A long hill made the first mile tough and then the terrain settled into a roller coaster ride. At least the shoulders were in good condition. Animal carcasses covered every quarter mile, which reminded me of how harsh life could be. We never saw one house in the first half of the day. Luckily, a rest area had a pump and I had a long, mid-day drink. At 30 miles, Howard began walking one and riding one to take the pressure off me. We limped into the café at Mastadon after 38 miles in 100 + degree heat.

On one of his mile walks Howard told me why he wasn't too worried about me drinking when I was thirsty.

"Misty, do you remember a conversation I had with an ancient Texan near Lake Grapevine over a year ago?" Howard asked. "I asked if he knew anything about how long a horse could go safely without water."

The old man had chuckled before answering the question. He told Howard that many years ago he had to be go somewhere in August. He packed up his mule and the three of them had left camp at daybreak. Neither his horse nor his mule had any water before they stopped at near midnight.

"Midnight!" Howard exclaimed. "You must have made some 70-80 miles." The old man agreed on the distance.

"Mind you," he continued, "I re-hydrated the horses for the next two days."

On the basis of that story, Howard knew I could go all day, if necessary, and not suffer any permanent damage.

Howard obtained some hay and grain for dinner somehow and that made life bearable. The flies buzzed all over me until Howard came to my rescue with the fly spray. Even so, they tormented by just being all around me.

Howard had dinner in the air-conditioned bar-café. He greeted me at dusk and checked me over. The flies still flew all around me and he gave me a few more squirts of spray. Really, only the darkness made them bearable.

Howard did not wait for the café to open before hitting the road. We were warming up in the first quarter mile, when Howard stopped short and whistled.

"See that snake Misty?" Howard asked. "A car just ran over a three-foot rattlesnake. They can kill you so don't mess around."

I eyed the dead snake on the road and made a mental note to stay clear. Snakes were not the only danger. The number of animal holes on the shoulder increased that day. If it is not one thing on this journey, it's another.

After three hours, Howard rode me into the Dinosaur Park Headquarters. After finding me a couple of buckets of water, five couples on big motorcycles invited him to lunch. Two of the ladies gave me apples and I was able to stand in the shade of the picnic area trees. It was a pleasant surprise break and snack in the middle of this desert.

A few minutes later, we rode into the dusty town of Dinosaur and trotted to the only place in town with grass--the Colorado Welcome Center. I am not sure if Howard trusted me more or was too tired, but he not only stripped my gear as usual, he took off my bridle. I spent the next four hours mostly eating grass and taking one long nap on the cool, green grass. Howard dutifully picked up my poop.

After talking to a man as the center closed, Howard led me across the street to the village's park. He secured me to the bicycle rack, before crossing the street to eat his supper. The place had all these big replicas of dinosaurs but I knew they were not alive.

CHAPTER 8—BURNING INFERNO OF UTAH

Howard packed me up before daybreak and led me to the Miner's Café down the street. Unfortunately, it did not open until seven and so we got a late start at 7:40 AM. The shoulders were so bad Howard had me riding in the ditch most of the first 20 miles. I hated that. Between the bottles, cans and other junk, I dodged animal holes and all the irregularities of the earth.

Howard was leading me when "CREATURES – DANGER" entered my brain and I slammed to a stop. 'What were they?' I asked myself as I eyed six little monsters only 50 yards away. I snorted and turned my head, which caused the six antelopes to run wildly towards the surrounding hills. Howard laughed but it wasn't funny to me.

Howard let me walk beside him without holding onto the reins. It was extra work for him and he now trusted me enough to be without control, even beside the highway.

Moments out of Dinosaur, a sign read, "WELCOME TO UTAH." As I soaked in the brown and gray desert scenery, I was not troubled or worried.

Our level of trust had become a source of comfort in this endless journey across America. That trust would be tested in the near future. It deepened from days when Howard walked when he could have ridden me. That trust came from his constant, soothing voice at times when I was scared of animals that might attack me, or so I thought. My trust in him came from knowing that he would do whatever it took to obtain water and feed for me. He would save my life from attack by mountain lions if needed. Along this endless ride, I felt his weight drop 15 pounds as he oftentimes went hungry because we camped out miles from towns.

It was a kind of loneliness out there in the middle of nowhere that took his breath away. The sunsets dazzled with every color one could imagine. They sprayed shadows across the mountains and prairies. They reflected from colossal snow-capped peaks. Each day, we broke camp before dawn and rode west away from stunning sunrises. Oftentimes, Howard turned in the saddle and shared in words what he saw in those light banners streaking across the morning sky. At the end of the day, mighty thunderheads boiled into the heavens painted with gold, pink, purple and orange. Everywhere we rode, Howard described the wonder of it all. He talked to himself how it might have been in Daniel Boone's or the mountain man Jim Bridger's day.

Those men depended on a horse to carry them across the land.

From the rider Howard was in Georgia to the seasoned cowboy he had become made the difference in my ride and my experience. I know in the past from wars to ranches and farms, many horses suffered poor even brutal treatment by their riders. I thank my lucky stars that Howard was one of those cowboys that thought about his horse first. It meant that I would give my best to further his efforts in this journey from one ocean to another.

As good as he was, sometimes there was nothing he could do about our situation in the burning inferno known as Utah. In that agonizing desert, a man's mouth became so dry, he couldn't spit. The sweat dried in salt patches on his shirt. Howard's face turned into grim determination. The sweatband on his cowboy hat cracked in the relentless heat. I felt the heat cook my hooves at ground level where it felt like walking along at the end of a woman's hair dryer. The sand burned hotter than a farrier's furnace. The merciless sun baked the asphalt into heat waves in the distance. Above us, vultures soared in the skies searching for road kill. If given the chance, they would gladly feast on Howard or me. This desert land was not fit for man or horse. Yet, Howard pulled down the brim of his hat and pushed forward. I followed this cowboy because he was a Long Rider and I was his horse.

I traveled 18 miles without water as there was nothing until we reached the Utah Welcome Center at Jensen. I was munching grass when a woman came out and said I had to stay off the grass...something about breaking a sprinkler system.

I waited on the concrete while Howard ate lunch. I was happy he kept it to 30 minutes. He still had a tendency to get long-winded. Fifteen miles later, Howard led me to the feed store on the east end of Vernal. I received a nice shower from the female employees, while others filled up my grain bag. A mile or so later Howard received permission to stay behind the biker bar. After Howard set up the picket line and his tent, he led me across the street to the best grass in town. For the next three hours, I filled my tummy with grass, courtesy of the state prison system. Howard rested in the grass; anywhere he could find shade from the sun.

Howard surprised me the next morning with the sweetest words I know--"rest day." The owner of the bar found me a bale of hay and combined with the grain and the shade of the big trees, life could not get much better. The only thing that bothered me was my hooves. The new shoes I received near Denver were recessed a half inch from the edge of my toes and the leading edges wore off rapidly. I don't know why the farrier did not put them out to the edge like all the others did. It did not hurt but in this land of not much, I did not want to go lame.

Knowing my love for fresh grass, in the afternoon Howard again led me across the street. I had been happily munching for two hours, when a police car stopped. Howard who had been lying down on the grass near me got up and met the officer.

"Afternoon officer. What's up?" Howard asked.

"Well, the prison guards noticed you and your horse getting a little too close to the front gate," the officer said. "That, plus the gun on your hip, well they would like you to leave the area."

"Oh man," Howard said. "I am sorry. I forgot about the gun. As a retired police officer, I don't give it enough thought."

With that he took my reins and led me back to my picket line behind the bar.

Howard left a short time later for dinner. While he was gone, a bunch of vehicles drove by me and made me nervous. I pranced around in circles trying to see everything. After a few minutes I found myself with no slack in the rein and I could hardly move my neck. That is how Howard found me an hour later.

"Oh geez Misty," Howard said. "What in the world caused you to tie yourself up in knots?"

He ran over and unsnapped the rein so I could move my head again. My neck ached from having it locked in the same position. I shook it to get the kinks out. This caused a worried look on Howard's face. It took me the rest of the night to make it feel right.

At daybreak, Howard led me four miles through the long, skinny town. Breakfast was another concrete park job for me. Ouch! I was eager to get going by the time Howard mounted up. Without asking for permission, I bolted into a gallop, while Howard was still getting settled into the saddle.

"Whoa!" he ordered and pulled back hard on the reins.

I reluctantly came to a stop.

"Misty you can't take off like that," Howard said. "I don't care if you change speeds but you don't start until I say so. Clear?"

Okay, okay. I am sorry. It won't happen again. I know Howard has to get situated in the saddle before I take off in a full gallop. I certainly don't want Howard to fly out of the saddle and break his neck in the middle of nowhere. I'd be stranded and have no idea what would happen to me if he died.

The shoulders became excellent again and we made good time with less stress. Arriving in Gusher, Howard learned that the only café in town was closed on Mondays. However, moments later, when he asked a woman in her yard for water, she invited us to lunch. I spent the hour in a paddock with grain and hay, while I saw Howard feast on burgers, chips and melon. Fortune smiled upon us once again.

As we neared the city of Roosevelt, clouds covered up the sun for the first time since Berthoud Pass. It was only psychological relief, as the temperature remained near 100 degrees of scorching heat. Howard led me toward a saddle and western store--parking me next to a trailer with three horses and two dogs.

"Where you coming from Paint?" one of the horses snorted.

"Georgia," I replied.

"Georgia? Never heard of it. Where is that?" the quarter horse asked.

"Two thousand miles back that way," I answered using my head to point to the southeast.

"You have got to be joking," the stallion snorted in disbelief. "Nobody rides a horse that far."

"He does," I responded pointing to Howard coming back through the door.

Howard bought some carrots at the grocery store. At the west edge of town, Howard bought 50 pounds of feed, giving me some on the spot. He poured most of 40 pounds into three bags and put them in the cantle bag. "Ughhh." The weight reminded me of Georgia and the 44 pounds we had started out with. On the plus side, I knew the weight was grain for me and not unnecessary junk for Howard. We trotted down the highway for a mile, before Howard led us into the parking lot of Cody's Café.

Howard spent the next two hours scrounging grass for me at the trailer sites behind the café. At dusk, Dan came by and gave me all the hay I could eat that night. Bless you sir! He told Howard he owned the tire store next door and had noticed us trying to find grass. Combined with the grain, I slept on a full stomach.

Twenty-five pounds of grain remained next morning, which Howard loaded into the normal 10-pound cantle bag. The first few miles had good shoulders but Howard held me down to a trot, probably because of the weight. After a water break for me in Myton, we encountered a brand new road with terrible shoulders. I was forced to spend the next 20 miles in the ditch. My mind grew weary trying to spot snakes, holes and bottles. Once Howard jerked me hard to the left because I had not seen a two by four with large nails sticking out. Howard also spent time knocking bugs off my neck that the fly spray did not stop.

Howard stripped my gear at the east end of Duchesne and for the first time brought out a sign which read: "HAY." I munched on the grass at the post office while he held out the sign to about nine trucks pulling horse trailers. When they did not stop, he pulled a few dollars out of his wallet and held up both to the trailers. Still he had no luck. Eventually a local man stopped by to direct us to the local fairgrounds for the night. An hour later, he drove up with lots of hay for me and a cold soda for Howard. Howard told the man he was for sure going to heaven.

We slept in a covered, 60 X 100-foot arena, passing a quiet night.

After breakfast at the town's café, I discovered that there was only seven pounds of grain left to carry. That was good because my hooves caused me some discomfort. I had lost a lot of toe in the past two days. I took off at a lope but after only a mile or so, it hurt too much and I dropped down to a trot the rest of the day. Howard cursed the farrier back in Colorado but that did not improve the situation.

Around midday, we had to cross a tall bridge over the Strawberry River. Howard stopped me in the middle to admire the scenery. I was surprised to see so much water in this desert.

The village of Fruitland turned out to be more of a gas station/grocery store than a village. Luckily, the owner let us stay the night. He had watered a small section of lawn where I spent the rest of the day and night mowing it down. Howard fed me the last of the grain, completing my dinner. Howard needed to see a farrier as soon as possible. The night cooled since we approached another mountain pass.

The next day's 18 miles climbed up hill. After a quick breakfast for Howard at a gas station, I was barely able to manage a walking pace for the rest of the day. The stench of rotting deer carcasses filled my nose most of the morning and afternoon.

"I am so sorry about your hooves girl," Howard said. "I could hurt that farrier who did this to you. As you can see, we are in the middle of nowhere and we won't see a farrier until we reach the bottom of the pass tomorrow. Hang in there girl. I'll take as much walking as I can."

With those words, Howard began to ride one mile, lead me one mile. This allowed me to munch on the first roadside grass in hundreds of miles. With his weight off me and back to only 10 pounds of pack, the pain was bearable.

Howard led me down an embankment to get some water in the Strawberry Reservoir Lake. He took off his boots and playfully splashed me in the lake to cool me off. It was a nice break for both of us, taking our minds off our troubles, if only for a few minutes.

An hour later, I spotted a bunch of my equine buddies on the left side of the highway near a barn. Howard did too and I was soon put in a stall by myself with lots to eat and drink. I was grateful for the short day.

Howard disappeared into one of the nearby cabins. Near dusk, I saw him hanging laundry over the railings. He had become quite ripe in the past few days and I was glad he could take a shower and have some clean clothes.

The resort was located at the summit of the pass and it was all down hill the next day. Howard led me the whole 16 miles to a ranch near Heber City. As my hooves were now causing pain with every step, his sacrifice was much appreciated.

At the ranch Jim took one look at my hooves and informed Howard that he did not have the technical expertise to fix the problem. He did call his friend Cody who agreed to come out the next day and take a look.

Howard met Peggy a few moments later and I could tell from her voice that life was not good that day.

"You and your horse are most welcome to stay a few days," she said. "Put her in a pen over there and you can sleep in the basement of the house. There is a bed and shower."

"Is there anything I can do to help you, Peggy?" Howard asked.

"Well," she replied. "My full-time hand was arrested last night and I have no idea when he will return. I have 28 stalls to clean and I have to be ready for some folks coming out to buy a horse."

"I'd be happy to clean the stalls for you," Howard volunteered.

"You are a guest but if you would do that, I would be most grateful," she said.

A few minutes later I saw Howard disappear into the main barn. Throughout the rest of the day,

I spotted him cleaning stalls, emptying the poop buckets and in the evening, he helped Peggy feed the 40 horses on the ranch. It was like being back on the ranch in Chattanooga.

Around noon the next day, Howard led me over to the main barn where Cody the farrier was setting up. He whistled when he saw how much toe I had lost. He removed the old shoes and began sizing me up for new ones.

"I'll try to make these as perfect as possible Howard but Misty might be lame for weeks," he said. "We won't know until she puts pressure on the new shoes."

Cody got all four shoes red hot and then burned them into my hoof. The smoke and smell were bad but I wasn't ruffled by it. Ninety minutes later, I had new shoes. Howard couldn't look any more dejected. Both of us could see that the toes of the front shoes weren't touching any of my hooves for three inches. The back ones were almost as bad.

"What's the damage on the shoes?" Howard asked, pulling out his wallet.

"I understand you've been helping Peggy the past two days, cleaning stalls and such," Cody replied. "So one hand washes the other and no charge."

Howard protested but was unable to give Cody any money.

Howard led me to the arena and asked me to trot. The shoes felt good and the pain was not there. I went from trot to lope, until Howard told me to stop. He jumped on bareback and we trotted for five minutes. His weight did not cause any pain. I was ready to go.

The next morning a reporter interviewed Howard and took photos. Gingerly, Howard loaded me up and then eased into the saddle. I trotted off briskly and upon reaching US 40, I broke into a fast lope. Howard yelled and screamed like we had just crossed the Mississippi River Bridge. I guess he was happy that I was okay and running. Indeed, Cody had worked a miracle and I was sound again.

Two miles later Howard parked me on grass at the café. He was talking on his cell phone, when three Utah State Troopers approached us. Howard greeted them with "Morning guys."

The lead trooper asked, "Did you know that there is a local ordinance here in Heber City against open carry?"

Howard's face lost a little color before he asked, "Can I fix it now?"

"Sure," came the reply.

Howard dropped the clip, popped out the round, removed the barrel from the frame, emptied the clip, placed the clip in my pack, took off his red bandana, stuffed it into the magazine area and re-holstered the frame into the holster.

"Am I legal now?" Howard asked.

The troopers were all smiling at the bandana sticking out of the frame and they agreed he was now legal.

"Thanks guys," Howard said. "I am a retired police officer and appreciate the heads up."

After breakfast, Howard was walking me through town, when three local officers stopped us and engaged Howard in conversation. At the city limits Howard put his semi-automatic pistol back together.

"Wow, Misty," Howard said. "Was I lucky or what to run into those troopers. I think those three city officers would have arrested me. They were none too friendly."

Howard said that with a sigh of relief.

We made a long, slow climb for the next couple of miles, as the road became a four lane, busy highway. The hot sun baked us like a branding iron on a horse's hide.

After a sharp downhill, Howard led me off the road and onto an old railroad bed.

I took off fast and enjoyed the lack of traffic and noise. The bed was hard dirt and a joy to be on. I spied a hawk perched on a large mound of dirt. As I was admiring its beauty, I stepped into a gopher hole, stumbled and crashed into the dirt. I skinned my nose again pretty badly but otherwise I was okay. Even there, I had to pay attention as much as anywhere.

Howard brought me to a halt and jumped off to check me over.

"I am sorry girl," Howard said. "I was looking at the hawk, instead of the road. It won't happen again."

The rail trail wound its way next to a small stream that split the two directions of an expressway. Howard led me down to it for a big drink but he went thirsty. He had emptied his water bottle two hours before we reached the next town of Wanship. With the temperature again well into the 100s running out of water was never a good thing.

After providing me with a five-gallon bucket of water, Howard spent two hours in the café in Wanship. As he saddled me up, he lamented the lack of grass for me to eat. I smiled at Howard's comment because I had smelled an alfalfa field just around the corner.

"Misty! Are you lucky or what?" he exclaimed when he saw the acre of lush grass.

He stripped me and let me chew on the rich grass until near dark. Leaving me for a few minutes, he returned with my grain bag full of oats. I had gone from nothing to a great meal in only 50 yards!

Howard pitched his tent in the parking lot of the rail-trail and I was short-tied with reins just looped around a pole for the night.

Howard broke camp well before dawn and we made three miles before we saw the sun break over the eastern hills. Howard was walking me over a rail-trail, wooden bridge, when "DANGER - UNKNOWN CREATURE" message hit my brain, as I noticed a large animal a few feet off the bridge. My flight instinct caused me to turn violently, nearly knocking Howard into the stream.

"Easy girl," Howard said softly. "It's just a deer."

He held me fast and indeed, I saw the deer bound away from us, probably more scared than I was.

After 10 miles, Howard left the trail to eat in Coalville. Walking on Main Street, we came to a long table of food outside the city hall. Howard parked me under a tree, as he chowed down on the food prepared by the local Lions Club.

A woman came over with her children and gave me an inspection.

"This horse is well-cared for and obviously brushed every day," she declared.

I chuckled to myself. Well-cared for yes, but my coat had not felt a brush, since we left Denver!

I was not happy to see him politikin' because the day grew hotter. Finally, after an hour, we departed.

We had gone a short ways when Howard suddenly jerked my reins hard to the right. This caused me to slow down and then see the large dog that appeared about to bite me on the leg. I looked him in the eye and pinned my ears, causing the now barking dog to back off. Howard had me turn around and force the dog back in his yard. The sneak attack had been handled without injury. A young lad grabbed the dog and I thought the incident closed. As soon as we left the driveway, the kid let the dog loose again. Howard swung me around again and again I drove the dog back into his yard. This time Howard yelled that he would have me kill the dog, if the owner let him loose again. Those words ended the problem.

The road ended forcing us to go on expressway I-84. Howard led me to the entrance but the roadway was covered by a cattle guard. Howard began to mumble and complain. At that moment, a pickup truck came up the exit and Howard walked us over.

"You wouldn't happen to have any plywood would you?" Howard asked.

"As a matter of fact I have one sheet in the bed," the young man replied.

"Would you mind if I used it get my horse over the cattle guard?"

A minute later, I walked over the plywood and onto the freeway entrance.

For the second time I had to ride on the shoulder of a busy, noisy freeway. It really wasn't much different and the shoulders were quite good for traction and comfort. East of Morgan Howard stopped me to gaze on the unusual rock formation called "Devil's Slide."

Trying to get off the expressway at Morgan proved harder than entering. Howard tried for half an hour to locate plywood, before giving up.

"Misty, I saw a partial tear in the fence a short distance back," Howard said. "We will have to try that."

The fence had been torn by the landowner and it was big enough for me to squeeze through. Trouble was that there was a tiny stream to cross over and the concrete path over it was only four feet wide. Howard pushed his foot onto the base of the wire and urged me onto the ledge. After my rear legs were through, he stepped up, trying to get around and in front of me. I looked back to see how he was managing which caused my neck to knock him into the two-foot deep water. I thought he would get mad at me but he just led me from the steam laughing at the situation.

After Howard ate a late lunch at the local café, he took me a mile to the fairgrounds. Howard was letting me munch on the short grass, when a man came over and ordered me off. 'Is that guy from New York City or what?' I thought.

Being forced off the grass, Howard decided to explore the many stalls.

"Ka-ching Misty!" Howard exclaimed.

He had found many flakes of hay and pounds of grain left by the fairgoers last weekend. I just dove into the stuff. A short time later, a woman brought more grain, which Howard poured into my grain bag for tomorrow.

Howard threw a bunch of hay into the arena for the night. However, after he pitched his tent, I spent most of the night near it. Once I urinated and Howard woke up screaming because it was splattering into his tent! Ooops! It was so hot; he had not put the rain fly up. Eventually, I rested near the tent and felt secure enough to sleep.

"It is going to be a long one, girl," Howard informed me as he broke camp in the darkness. After he walked me a mile through town, we rode three miles to the Stoddard café arriving at sunrise.

Howard offered me the last of the grain, while he had his pancakes and coffee. Emerging an hour later, he chuckled and smiled.

"I learned something very important this morning for our travels through Utah," he said. "Namely if you tell people you eat crickets every day, they will think well of you."

I was skeptical and would wait until I saw him eat the first one.

At Enterprise, we moved onto the expressway again. The canyon became narrower as the morning progressed. We approached a curvy bridge that was long and had no breakdown lane. Howard dismounted and led me to its beginning. He waited until no traffic was coming and he ran me as fast as possible across the bridge. Looking back, we both saw traffic bearing down on us. He positioned me as close to the edge as possible, causing him to stand in the traveled lane. I knew I had to stand absolutely still because any movement on my part would shove him into the path of the cars and trucks.

After waiting for a dozen or so trucks to scream by, he ran us off the bridge. His trust in me was enormous and I did not let him down. Three times that morning we landed in such a predicament, where we both needed nerves of steel.

Finally, we rode off I-84 and proceeded north onto US 89. The shoulders featured tall grass and after a short ride, Howard dismounted and walked most of the next six miles through Ogden. We stopped at a burger place for lunch and bless Howard; he parked me on the grass and under a tree! Howard found water for me six times during that grueling 38-mile day in 100-degree heat.

Leaving North Ogden, Howard began the ride one, walk one mile routine we always did after 30 miles.

"Good news, girl," Howard said. "I met two guys at the Summit Pass who invited us to stay with them. Just a few more miles, sweetheart."

It was a comfort to know that tonight would be spent at a ranch.

It was dark when we turned down a side street in the village of Willard. A few minutes later Howard led me into Russ's barn with its shelter, hay and grain and a few bovines for company. I enjoyed all that after Howard gave me a thorough shower.

I observed Russ cook Howard a barbecue dinner, followed by lots of conversation and laughing. He told me later that he slept in a 'bunkhouse' owned by Ralph. The bunkhouse was described as something out of the Old West, complete with tons of antiques.

The next day Russ fed me more hay and grain. I did not see Howard until noon.

"Rest day girl," he told me.

I was surprised we did not take two rest days. As the mooing of the Angus cattle kept me company, I rested in the shade, ate and then did it all over again.

The welcomed rest ended at daybreak as Howard saddled me up and we walked back to US 89. We made good time and arrived for breakfast in Brigham City. Howard found a café with a split rail fence and inside there was grass. Later, a local newspaper reporter stopped us for pictures and interview.

Howard pointed us up I-15, which featured great shoulders. We were nearing Tremonton exit, when Utah Trooper Kanno rolled in behind us. Howard must have sensed something because he turned, saw the patrol car, stopped and hopped off. Howard and the trooper had a nice conversation, giving me an unexpected break. After 10 minutes or so we loped off the expressway and a few minutes later I was parked across the street from a café.

A few miles later, I saw the fairgrounds and knew we were done for the day. I was relieved to have an average 24-mile day. Howard gave me a shower and hooked me to the infield fence. He spent 15 minutes moving a few poles, which would allow me to roam the 10 acres during the night. The infield offered a water tank full of delicious, green looking water. Howard tried hard to force me to drink fresh water from the tap but the green water tasted so much better. Finally, he gave up.

After the sun went down, 25 of my horse friends show up. They carried members of the sheriff's posse, practicing for an upcoming rodeo fair. I had given up on grain as Howard made final preparations to sleep. Then a small truck showed up and after a short chat, I had some great grain, courtesy of Russ and Ralph from Willard. Thanks guys.

It was hours before dawn and still nearly 80 degrees when Howard stirred from his tent and broke camp in the dark. He walked me almost to the expressway, before hooking me to a light pole in front of the café. It was before the crack of dawn when Howard came out and saddled me up. He put on his miner's light, turned it on to the strobe feature and put it around his neck, facing backwards. I knew at that moment we were about to ride in pitch black.

The traffic was light, the shoulders good and I was able to see okay with the star light. We traveled 10 miles before the rays of the sun hit us. The desolate view did nothing to lift my spirits. The temperature quickly rose to 100 as we loped and walked through this desert.

Howard had told me that Russ and Ralph were going to find us today, bringing lunch and water. Almost like a mirage, they were parked at an exit waiting for us about 25 miles into the day. We ate under the bridge. Both of us were starved and thirsty and we spent a good hour savoring our feast in the barren wastelands. Russ and Ralph promised to deliver more hay and grain to the evening campsite in Snowville. Howard gave them both a big hug, before letting them go.

The sun drilled into us as we plodded ahead. Once again the stench of rotting carcasses pierced our noses--adding to our misery. After 28 miles, Howard began the walk-one ride-one routine. He sensed my fatigue. The sun sucked the energy out of me.

In the late afternoon we exited the freeway and into the small town of Snowville, Utah. After we arrived at the campgrounds and Howard dropped off our gear, we walked back to the post office for some munch time. Later Howard grabbed dinner while I stood on the asphalt. After I made a poop pile, a zillion flies arrived to have their dinner. They drove me crazy, but Howard walked out and we left.

Back at the RV Park, Howard showered and chatted with a couple from Texas as the darkness deepened. Howard hooked me up to a picnic table next to his tent on the driving range. Going to bed with a full stomach made the hard, 39-mile day have a good ending.

The next morning we had to go back a half-mile into the village for Howard to eat. I stood in the same spot and when I pooped, Howard came out and scooped it up and took it to the road.

"I was a bad cowboy yesterday Misty," he said. "I should have cleaned up your mess and I didn't. I apologized to the folks inside. I was just so tired last night, I wasn't thinking straight. I have some lousy news for today's ride. We are looking at 36 miles of desert, sun, heat and no shade. We'll have to cowboy up again."

Oh great, I love it when he tells me to 'cowboy up'. He forgets that I'm a horse.

CHAPTER 9—IDAHO ON NO GRASS, NO SHADE, NO RELIEF

We had just crossed into Idaho when Howard reined me up for an RV stopped on the side of the expressway.

"Anything I can do to help?" Howard asked the couple.

"The motor overheated and we are just going to wait for it to cool off. Thanks anyway," the man replied.

The two chatted five minutes before we loped off.

An hour later Howard gave out a whoop, as we read the sign "WELCOME TO IDAHO" rest area ahead. I savored the cool water there as I ate the last of the grain from yesterday. Lots of people came up and chatted with Howard who bragged about what a great horse I was. I wish I could have told them what a cowboy he was.

Every day in every way possible, his sacrifices kept me healthy.

Reluctantly, after a 30-minute break we loped off into the bleak, sun-baked landscape. Though I had lost five pounds of grain, Howard carried a whole gallon of water away from the rest area. In the first mile, we endured several, stinking animal carcasses and then not another living thing the rest of the day. A 25-mph headwind sucked the energy and water out of both of us.

The 36-mile day to the truck stop in Sublett came to a close late in the afternoon. That was when all the drama started—caused by my acute thirst. I had drunk no water in 26 miles. A cattle guard blocked our way, so Howard had to tie me up to the barbed wire fence. He ran to the truck stop returning with a five-gallon bucket of water. I began screaming at him to hurry up with the water and pawed the ground in front of me. Seconds later, I hooked my right hoof in the barbed wire fence and was unable to move. I screamed louder at Howard to help me.

Softly his voice rang in my ears, "Easy girl. I'll get you loose. Easy sweetheart. You know I will take care of you."

He dropped the bucket of water and walked over to me. He already had his work tool out and quickly cut the wire on both sides, freeing me. I calmed down and nickered for the water.

As I sucked down the five gallons as fast as I could, Howard lifted up my hoof and worked the wire out. He retied me to the fence and ran for another five gallons. Upon his return, he only let me have a sip at a time.

"Misty, this idea of you staying out here is too dangerous," Howard said. "I am going to cut the fence, let you in and then repair the fence."

He cut about five strands of wire and pushed down the bottom ones with his boots, before leading me through. I stepped over the fence but my left rear caught a strand and I was hooked again. Howard had me free in no time and we walked the short distance to the truck stop.

Howard spent nearly two hours in the café. His long face signaled me he had had no luck finding any food for me. He led me to some brown grass near the truck parking but it wasn't worth eating. Desperate, we moved down a row of trailers and YES, between the last two there was tall, lush grass. Nobody was home so Howard just unhooked me and lay down on his side. In two hours I ate almost all the grass on that spot.

We left at first light but the day boiled over quickly, reaching 104 degrees. The wind continued sucking us dry. The expressway rest area after 20 miles was most welcome. There was no grass but at least I had water. We passed a large sign warning of sandstorms and I was glad we had not encountered that problem.

Just past the rest area, Howard stopped for a van that had a shredded left rear tire. The man trying to change it hobbled around on a cane.

"Can I give you a hand mister?" Howard inquired.

"I'd be grateful," the man from Colorado, Beau, replied.

Howard short-tied me to a reflector pole for an hour, while he used jacks and blocks of wood to fix the problem. Beau had been shot while working as a narcotics cop and used a wheel chair on most days. Though the sun cooked me, I knew Howard would not leave this man until the job was finished.

Beau and Howard decided to meet up at the first exit and have dinner but we never saw Beau again.

We were near Burley, when a truck pulling a horse trailer eastbound pulled into the median and the driver called out to us. Howard hopped off and led me into the median. "Smokey" provided me with a big drink of water and then a nice grain snack. He finished off his hospitality by filling my grain bag! The unrelenting misery of the 104-degree day was ignored for a few minutes as yet another stranger helped us out.

As the exit Howard wanted came into view, I felt the grain splash over my rump and tumble onto the highway. Somehow, the zipper had come loose, as Howard had carried the pack on his back. Moments later Howard screamed at the world, as he realized, too late, the loss of the precious grain. My evening feast was not to be.

We took the first exit off the expressway and headed for the gas pumps. As Howard stripped my gear, a horse trailer appeared at the station. Grabbing the empty blue bag, Howard walked over and, oh joy, returned with a full one. The horse equivalent of a steak and baked potato were back on the evening's menu.

I happily munched on grass near an RV park when I noticed a brown cloud far off to the east. 'Wow', I thought, it must be one of those sandstorms that the sign had warned about. Twenty minutes later

Howard let out a scream, as he grabbed my blankets, placed them next to me and stepped on them. And then it hit.

Sand particles and other debris slammed into my right side stinging me like a hundred bees. Howard took off his bandana and covered my left eye, which already had some sand in it. He hugged my neck, whispered that we would get through this together, shut his eyes and crouched behind me.

After a 29-mile day and the worst 103 miles of the journey, the sandstorm added the final insult to my week. For 45 minutes the sand stung me all over. There was no shelter for Howard to take me. At least my eye was protected.

As the storm subsided, the Zak the manager of the RV Park came out and offered us a place. Howard led me past several limbs which had cracked off the trees. The 50-mph wind had done some damage. Howard told me later that the storm had knocked over trucks and trailers on the Interstate.

Howard gave me a good shower to start the late afternoon. The RV Park offered lots of grass and I relaxed in the green. With Howard watching, I rested and fell into a deep sleep. Howard was still a sentinel when I awoke an hour later. Since the mosquitoes were thick, Howard sprayed me before hooking me up to a small tree.

The couple next to us invited Howard over for a cold drink and later for dinner. I was happy to see him go into the shower room and get his own.

Long before dawn the mosquitoes attacked me and I nickered loudly, hoping to wake Howard up.

It took a few tries and finally, he poked his head through the tent.

"Go back to sleep Misty!" he ordered.

I screamed at him to come over with fly spray. He must have noticed me swishing my tail like mad because a minute later he was by my side.

"Sorry girl," he apologized as he sprayed me all over, relieving me of the torment of those little bloodsuckers.

He broke camp and we hit the road at daybreak. We had just left the RV Park and were on the bridge over the interstate, when I saw a monstrous bird wing coming up low and slow from the rear. I knew a bird that big could kill me. I tried to run but Howard's grip on the reins was too tight. I was ready to jump off the bridge, when the truck with a flapping tarp passed us.

"Misty, Misty girl. It's okay. It's just a tarp, not a dragon," Howard cried in a low, steady voice. I was relieved and calmed down.

We loped into the town of Declo but the only café was closed. We traveled another few miles into Burley, where Howard parked me on the concrete while he had breakfast.

"We are here for the day Misty," Howard said. "We both deserve a short day."

Howard led me to a city park, which was full of teens on skateboards. He turned me loose to munch on the green grass, while he rested, using the saddle as a backrest.

Hours later a police officer approached Howard and asked what was going on. The cop said we had to move because some people had complained that I might hurt the grass or something. He recommended the fair grounds a five-minute walk from the park.

Howard packed me up and we walked to the busy area of the entrance. The tall, green grass was all I needed plus shade! There was a rodeo that day and I became a one-horse petting zoo. At least 75 kids came up to pet me. I didn't mind, since I just kept eating. It did force Howard to stand up and ensure the little cowboys and cowgirls were safe.

After five hours Howard said we needed grain and he led me to the area where all the horse trailers were parked. A few minutes later my grain bag was full and I tore into the oats. As darkness descended, Howard set up his tent near the inside rail away from the trucks and trailers.

"I am going to get a little water before calling it a day Misty," Howard said as he headed over in the direction of the hose.

While he was gone, four deputies came over to his tent and looked inside with their flashlights. They surrounded him when he came back a few minutes later.

"Don't move a muscle!" one ordered.

Howard froze like a statue.

"Is that a gun on your hip?"

"Yes, sir. It is the 9MM I carried as a police officer until I retired," Howard replied.

"Bill, take his gun," Bill stepped up and took Howard's pistol.

"You have a hunting license in Idaho? If not, you are in violation of the law."

"No sir," Howard said. "I don't have a hunting license. I was told one could carry open in Idaho."

"Are you connected with the rodeo? If not, you are trespassing."

"No, I am not with the rodeo. I am riding my horse across America."

"So, you are breaking two laws. As soon as I check with my sergeant, you are going to jail."

A few minutes later, the sergeant came up in a patrol car and the mean deputy briefed the command officer. You should have seen Howard's face go from depression to relief.

"Those are just two minor infractions," the man said. "Move him off fairground property, give him a verbal warning and return his pistol."

The mean deputy looked mighty disgusted as he emptied Howard's clip and gave him back the weapon. Howard holstered the gun, packed me up and we moved 150 yards to a fence in the parking lot. Howard placed me on a picket line, using the fence as the anchor points. As he pitched his tent, he muttered about what a narrow escape that had been. He was sure he would spend the night in jail and how he worried what would happen to me.

Bright and early the next day we walked to the center of town and the only place serving breakfast on a Sunday.

The rolling terrain was the only easy part of the day. A hard west wind blew in our faces plus the sun and heat. During a walk and munch Howard jerked me hard once. I had almost put my mouth on top of a two-foot long snake.

Just after midday, Howard stopped at a ranch to ask for grain. Zeb Bell and his wife took care of both of us. While I chewed on grain and hay, Dee Anne served up a hot meal and lots of ice-cold lemonade for Howard and Zeb. As we walked off the property, Howard let me know that later in the day Zeb would meet us for a TV interview in the town of Kimberly. The flat land of the "Miracle Valley" combined with good shoulders made the 34-mile day bearable.

True to his word, Zeb and the cameraman met us on the outskirts of Kimberly. We proceeded to a park for the six-minute taping. Howard put me behind a park bench, while he and Zeb sat. Toward the end of the taping I realized that the camera was not putting me on TV. So, I knocked over some rocks to move next to Howard on the bench. I was rewarded by the camera moving to put me in the show. Needless to say, Howard and Zeb were a bit startled. It wasn't like this was a one-man show! It was a horse and a man riding across America—and I was the horse. We need more respect for the horse—and I was going to get it one way or the other.

It was nearly dark when Howard walked out of the Chinese restaurant and led me to the only green grass in town; a former high school featured tall grass, which I devoured. I had been mowing down the grass for an hour when a woman talked to Howard. A few minutes later the woman drove away and Howard let out a sharp yelp.

"Misty girl, good news," Howard said. "Tink and her niece Teal have a small ranch on the outskirts of town and we are headed there now."

Since it was already pitch black, I was glad we had found shelter. That night I enjoyed a small paddock all to myself. Some equines in the next stall guarded me, allowing me to sleep long and deep. Howard told me later he slept on the couch after a great meal and shower.

We slept in that morning, not leaving until almost 9:00 AM. We had traveled less than a mile, when the TV camera filmed us riding and walking into Twin Falls. One day, I hoped Howard would allow me to see myself.

Howard's breakfast stop had me parked on the concrete of a café. At least it was covered against the sun. A few moments after leaving the café, Howard let me munch in the yard of an abandoned house for nearly an hour, before we walked to the city hall. Rebecca, a reporter for the local paper, interviewed him for over an hour. It was a shady break for me and I knew it was going to be a short day. YES!

Howard ate lunch at the burger joint near a busy intersection. He stopped at a gun store and came out wearing his pistol again. After nearly being arrested, he wasn't taking any chances. He bought a hunting license. Given the problems with dogs and the potential for cougars, I was glad to see it on his hip again.

On the west edge of town a man on a bicycle came up to us and stopped. Jim introduced himself and then invited us to his ranch to spend the night. As he bicycled, we followed him for two miles to the town of Filer. I stayed in a nice paddock for the night, except for the two loud mules next door.

Howard put out a generous helping of straight corn but I didn't care for it. I ate all the hay and with my mule buddies watching, I had another good night's sleep.

Howard came out the next morning in clean clothes, smelling fresh and clean-shaven. Jim showed us All-American hospitality. That day we had dozens of people wave and beep their horns. Howard said it was because we had been on TV last night, plus a big picture and story on us in the paper.

Howard opened the paper and showed me the large, color photograph of us on the sidewalk in Twin Falls.

"Do we make a cute couple or what?" Howard asked.

East of Buhl a truck stopped by and the driver wanted to talk to Howard. Bill and Valerie invited us to stay at their place west of town near the hot springs. Alice came over and gave me some carrots plus gave Howard a glob of cream, which he rubbed into my right hip muscle. I guess they thought it was injured.

Although I had slept well, I suffered the 'feel-me-no-goods'. I broke out of a lope several times that day. Howard got me plenty of water from the irrigation ditches, but something was wrong.

It was only a 20-mile day to the ranch and that was a relief. I was put into a unique area that could only be described as a hippie commune. I had freedom within the fence to see the old school bus, sheds, trailers and washers that covered the area. There wasn't any grass but Howard provided me with lots of hay and grain. The numerous small trees did provide shade from the blazing sun.

I did not sleep well that night. I was relieved when Howard told me the next morning that it was a rest day. I munched on the hay and stayed in the shade, as my stomach was still not right. Howard, Bill and Valerie ate meals outside and all seemed to enjoy long conversations.

We left early the next morning under cloudy skies. It was our first relief from the sun in weeks. I still didn't feel well but Howard said it was time to go. I loped when I could--trotted or walked--when I didn't feel well enough. Howard walked me more than usual, trying to take the stress off me.

"What is wrong girl?" he asked. "I gave you a day off with lots of good food and shade. I wish you could tell me."

We rode along US 30 all day. Around noon, I saw the most amazing sight. To my right, water gushed out of the middle of the rocks on the canyon walls. In a dozen places or more, it featured waterfalls where none should be. The water rushed down to the Snake River that we followed most of the day. As the roadway climbed hard, Howard jumped off and walked two miles. He is such a friend. US 30 took us into the small town of Bliss, where Howard stopped at an RV Park behind the café.

We spent the next five hours letting me eat the grass near the café and in the football practice field. A couple of teens came over and rubbed me. Suddenly one of them grabbed my bridle and began pulling me toward the road.

"Hold it!" Howard shouted.

The teen froze in his tracks.

"Let go of the bridle and get out of here," Howard commanded.

The three teens walked back to the road and vanished. That was weird.

At dusk, Howard fed me grain that a rancher had dropped off. While Howard ate his dinner, a little dog left a trailer and ran over to Howard's pack. He took off with two of Howard's plastic bags and ripped at them about 100 feet away. After Howard returned, he noticed the bags in the grass and muttered. After that, he always kept his stuff in the cantle bag and zipped up.

I spent the night on a picket line and enjoyed a good sleep. The way Howard arranged it; I was able to lie down, which always helped. When I awoke the next morning, my stomach felt good for the first time in three days.

The weather continued cloudy and not hot as we left early. We had to go up on I-84 again but I didn't mind. The shoulders were fantastic and I was full of energy. I loped hard all day, which made Howard smile. The rest area had no water but an RV couple supplied me with a couple of gallons.

I noticed the rain clouds coming at us and sure enough, we were in the middle of nowhere when it hit. Howard was nice enough to hop off and let me put my butt into the wind. We just huddled there on the shoulder getting soaked in the downpour. Howard had dropped off his raingear in Colorado to save weight and he was as soaked as I was.

Just east of Glenn's Ferry, road crews had demolished the eastbound lanes for resurfacing. I enjoyed eight miles of no traffic after Howard nudged me over to the empty eastbound lanes. Near the city limits, Howard angled me over to the eastbound bridge but a guide wire blocked our way. A construction foreman helped us out. He offered to have someone take down the wire but Howard said thanks but we would just cross on the westbound bridge. Too dangerous the man replied. As we trotted over to the bridge, Howard shouted back that this wasn't our first rodeo.

We trotted off the expressway and into town for food. Howard found me shade without much grass while he had lunch. I didn't feel comfortable and screamed at him just before he went into the café. He came out every five minutes as usual and every time I whinnied at him to hurry up.

After he watered me in the stream, which ran through the town, we rode back up the expressway. We trotted down hill from Glenn's Ferry to the exit for Hammett. We had traveled 27 miles and when Howard found grass at a trailer park near the exit, I munched for two hours.

After a short time, I noticed the blackening of the western sky. Howard who was dozing off in the grass near me never saw it. When he finally looked up, his eyes opened wide and he muttered something. He quickly threw the saddle on me. To mount up, he stepped on an old tractor tire in the grass. As he adjusted his seat, I heard bees buzzing. He had startled a whole hive. He must have figured it out too because he put the spurs into me as hundreds of angry bees chased us down the Old Oregon Trail Highway. I was never stung but it was close. Howard said a few choice words that cannot be repeated at this time.

Howard had me slow down after the bees were no longer a threat. However, a minute later we crossed a bridge, which gave us an unrestricted view of the western sky. It had turned black as night, except for the brown cloud near the ground.

"Holy smokes, Misty," Howard said. "It's another dust storm in front of the storm! We have to find shelter NOW!"

I too sensed the need for shelter and needed no encouragement to gallop off at top speed. The mile into town passed fast but we were racing right into the storm. We found no shelter on the edge of town. I continued galloping flat-out. If someone had seen us, they might think it was Clint Eastwood and his horse being chased by a band of outlaws. The inky blackness enveloped the heavens and filled me with fear. Thankfully, I was in tremendous condition after 2500 miles and running was what I liked to do.

I saw the swirling, brown cloud nearly upon us and still no gas station, no windbreak, nothing in sight. Then, like a miracle, a huge, open-front barn appeared on the left side of the road. As Howard brought me down to a trot, in order to safely cross over the slick asphalt, the 50-mph wind slammed into us from the right. Stinging sand blasted into my skin, hurting as if those bees had caught up. After trotting me across the pavement, I leaped into a dead gallop to reach the barn 50 yards away. We raced into the barn and I slammed to a stop in front of the bales of hay, leaving skid marks.

I was out of breath from the effort. Howard hopped off and led me around inside the cavernous structure, cooling me off. He couldn't stop praising me for my efforts and courage to run into such a storm. Gradually, my breathing came back down to normal. Howard let me munch some hay after he left two dollars on one of the bales.

The sandstorm lasted only about 10 minutes, replaced by a nasty thunderstorm. The boom of lightning strikes rang through the barn as the wind-driven rain pelted the roof like a machine gun. It was wonderful to be inside instead of out in the open at a time like that.

After the storm passed, we rode to the only café in town where Howard parked me near the window. I nickered loudly when he went inside to let him know I wasn't happy. After an hour, I screamed loudly and he came out. He led me through the village to a three acre grassy field owned by Dusty and Jake. Howard led me around the perimeter to make sure there were no gaps in the fence. Satisfied, he cut me loose. It was a peaceful ending after a day of too much excitement.

The heat and sun returned the next morning as we rode on the Interstate for most of the morning. Bleak, sun-baked vistas of brown hills extended to the horizon. We exited south of Mountain Home and made our way to Robin's house. Howard explained that Robin had been at the café yesterday and had arranged for lunch at his place. I was treated to grain and hay, while Robin served up a steak sandwich to Howard. I also enjoyed the shade of the huge tree in his yard.

Howard walked me most of the way to Liz & Eddie's ranch on the north side of Mountain Home. Several horses came over to greet me in their pasture. A round pen contained one of them and I went over to him.

"Why are you kept in here?" I asked.

"Less than a year ago I was captured by these humans," he replied. "I used to be a wild mustang, born and raised in an area near here."

"Wow. I have never met a horse born in the wild before. What's it like?" I asked.

"I guess I can compare the two lives. It was nice to have the freedom to just be a horse," he said. "I also know that they want to ride me one day. On the other hand, having perfect food and water is great. In addition, the vet has taken care of some problems I had. Both lives are good, I'd say."

After Howard vanished into the house for the night, I caught a great sleep, knowing my equines buddies would watch out for me.

"It is going to be another tough day Misty," Howard said. "It is 25 miles to water, not a bit of shade and no grass. Hopefully I will find you food at the end of the day but I won't promise."

Howard led me toward the expressway. I was happy to start the day with a full stomach and still at full weight. As tough as the last 500 miles had been, somehow Howard had kept me fed.

The sun crept into the eastern sky as we entered the freeway. We had traveled only a short distance, when I noticed a state trooper making a traffic stop on the eastbound lanes. Howard turned me toward the event. Moments later another eastbound car pulled in front of the first car, as the trooper was talking to the first driver.

Howard stopped and turned me perpendicular to the road to have the best view of what was going on.

"It's the second car stopping that has me concerned Misty," Howard said. "That is not normal. We'll wait here till all is okay."

I could not see if Howard had his hand on his gun, but I knew he did. After two to three minutes, the trooper had talked to both drivers.

"You all set?" Howard called out.

"Yes, thanks, all set," he shouted back.

As we turned to continue westward, Howard informed me, "You never know on traffic stops Misty. You never know. You have to take care of each other out here. Few others will."

An hour later new construction had left soft asphalt scattered all over the shoulder. Black, gooey stones stuck to my hooves and I could barely walk. Howard dismounted and led me into the ditch. Looking at the mess in my hooves made him grumble loudly.

"I'll have you cleaned out in a jiffy, Misty," he promised.

Fifteen minutes later and lots more grumbling I was ready to ride again.

A few miles later despite efforts to avoid the black stones, my hooves were filled up again. It took

Howard another 20 minutes in the boiling sun to fix me again. Mercifully, the construction ended and we made it to the truck stop about noon.

Howard looked in four places before he found water. It tasted funny but after 26 miles, it was nectar to me. He even found me shade under a small tree on the edge of a parking lot. When Howard was almost to the door of the café, I resigned myself to no lunch. Wait! Is that a horse trailer pulling up to the pumps? I watched him head to a small rig which was carrying those devil creatures, sheep. Moments later he was headed toward me with three flakes of alfalfa.

"Misty, bon appetite," Howard said with a smile.

My man Howard had come through again with a big help from another stranger.

An hour later Howard came out with some new friends, as I polished off the last of the hay.

"We'll expect you in two days at our place in Nampa," the man called Ted said.

"Thanks Ted for the invitation and the lunch," Howard said.

Howard was packing me up, when I noticed a horse trailer rig pull in across the street. Good old Howard, he noticed it too and crossed the road in seconds flat. Five minutes later my blue bag overflowed with oats and I entered horse heaven.

"It was the same story Misty," Howard said. "I asked the cowboy if I could buy some grain. He said no but you can have all you want. Do you realize I have only been able to pay for your feed once in 2,500 miles? People are so kind. When I was a cop, I knew that most people were good but dealing with criminals all the time, I had doubts. This trip has renewed my faith in people."

Howard let me eat most of the oats before we left. We were clearing the parking lot when a TV reporter showed up. It was a short interview-filming before we stepped back onto the expressway. The shoulder became horrible and Howard rode me in the ditch most of the time. Shortly after we stopped for water at a rest area, my rear left shoe fell off. Howard realized the problem and led me the last four miles to the first Boise exit. What a cowboy!

He let me graze on some good grass near a restaurant. He was preparing to camp there for the night, when I heard that distinctive sound of a diesel motor dying. I stopped munching long enough to see two ladies pop out of a king-cab truck. After chatting with Howard, they left. Howard's big grin signaled all I needed to know.

Sure enough, a few minutes later Susan and Deanna returned with a trailer. Five minutes later, I stood in a round pen with lots of grain, hay and water. Howard slept in the family's air-conditioned horse trailer. As I drifted off to sleep, I reflected what an amazing day it had been. Through 36 miles of desert, Howard and I had found strangers who took care of us.

The next morning Howard led me over to a shed where Jeremy tapped on a new shoe. Susan transported us both back to the café where the two had breakfast. The relentless August sun was roasting me when Howard emerged from the restaurant. I was happy to get moving. He rode less than a mile before he had to dismount and lead me on the grass next to the sidewalks of Boise.

Our urban trail ride took a good four hours before Howard led me out toward the expressway.

"Misty we need to make good time or we will be too late to stay with Ted and Missy tonight," Howard said.

Back on I-84, the traffic was heavy and the shoulder was mostly concrete. After 10 minutes Howard let out a long whistle and began grumbling. The shoulder disappeared due to construction and we had to ride on the expressway itself! Though Howard put me into a good eight mile per hour trot, the traffic soon stacked up behind me, as we caused a major traffic jam. Howard kept muttering that this was not a good thing. A mile later, two state trooper cars met us as the shoulder reappeared. The trooper was polite and firm as he showed us a gate to get off the expressway. I was sure I noticed that Howard's face was two shades redder and not from the hot sun.

Before shutting the gate the trooper turned to Howard.

"You must be the cowboy near Mountain Home who covered another trooper on a double traffic stop," he said. "On behalf of the other trooper, thanks for the backup."

"I was glad to be there and hey, let's be careful out there," Howard replied.

A few minutes later Missy showed up and led us to a house with a two-acre hay field. Howard gave me a long, refreshing shower, before turning me loose.

He returned a few minutes later with lots of grain. As he and Missy loaded up the car with my saddle, I realized he was leaving. I nickered loudly in protest which brought Howard over.

"Misty," Howard said. "I am staying with Ted and Missy tonight a few miles from here. I have checked your paddock and you'll be fine."

I resigned myself to the separation and returned to my grain as they drove off. The night was neither hot nor cold, signaling a change in the weather, I hoped.

The next morning we left in pleasant weather. It was mostly country along US 20 with great shoulders. We stopped at a ranch where a woman gave me oats and water. A few miles later Howard parked me at a café east of Caldwell. The area had grass and the lady in the motel filled a small bucket several times with water.

"Thanks for guarding my horse, ma'am," Howard sang out as we left.

"Anytime cowboy," she replied.

"I don't want to take you through Caldwell, so we will take the freeway for three miles girl."

Part of the 30-minute jaunt was strange. The shoulders and ditches had lush green grass, which Howard let me chew. Here in the desert the town watered expressway grass!

Mosquitoes started biting me west of town, causing Howard to bring out the bug spray. Just east of Notus, Howard stopped for a rest.

We had only been there a short time when Jeanna came up and offered to bring us home for the night.

She lived 14 miles away so they agreed to meet on the west edge of Notus. Howard walked me a mile or so until Jeanna returned with her trailer.

As the trailer rolled into a small farm, my eye grew huge as I saw a dead calf near the fence. I know we have to depend on strangers but this sight caused me to have fear. Howard led into a small paddock with two calves. Both of them tried to eat my grain. I pinned my ears trying to tell them to back off but either they did not understand or they ignored my warning. I smacked the black one on the head, nearly knocking him off his feet. The pair let me eat in peace.

CHAPTER 10—END OF THE TRAIL WITH LEWIS AND CLARK

Vaughn and Jeanna trailered us back to Notus and wished us luck. I felt good in the cool morning. I loped hard into the town of Parma where Howard bought me carrots. We waited on Main Street for half an hour so Howard could give our friend Zeb of Twin Falls a radio update on our trip. Howard rewarded my patience with a pound of carrots. An hour later, we approached the bridge that crossed the Snake River. Howard dismounted and walked me across. On the other side he screamed and hooted several times.

"Misty, do you see that "WELCOME TO OREGON" sign?" he asked pointing at the small sign. "This is the last state of our journey. We only have 450 miles to go to reach the Pacific Ocean. It is going to be another month of hard living and we will start it with five days off. We only have another month on the road."

I nickered and contemplated his words as he walked me through the town of Nyssa. We had come so far that it was surreal that he was talking of the trip coming to an end. I appreciated his explanation of coming events but I decided to continue taking it one step, one day at a time.

Oregon started out hard with a mile of concrete sidewalks followed by being tied up to the speaker box on concrete at a fast food joint! By the time we left, the boiling sun bore down in force. A lad of 10 tagged along beside us for two miles, peppering Howard with questions. The new state also produced a new hazard for me to watch out for; namely, large potatoes and onions, which had fallen off trucks and littered the shoulders. We passed streets like Onion Road, Siphon Circle and Tattle Tale Lane as we made our way along US 20 to Vale.

My muscles told me we had traveled a solid 36-mile day to reach the vet clinic in Vale before they closed at five. Howard gave me a soapy shower and massaged all the muscles in my body. He introduced me to some of the staff who would be taking care of me the next few days. Howard drove off with a friend while I munched on hay in my small stall.

The next five days were pleasant with perfect food and shelter. The staff walked me a few minutes each day to stretch my legs. A farrier came by one morning and gave me a new set of shoes. I missed my friend Howard but knew he would return. He showed up at midnight five days later. He said good-bye to his friend and came straight to me. I nickered a greeting as he led me out of the stall. He hugged me and told me how much he missed me. Though his presence meant the end of my little vacation, it also signaled the final push to the ocean. I thought of Scout, Leah and the good times we would have back at the ranch in Texas. I was eager to tell them all the adventures I had experienced!

The next morning we headed north on US 26 in bright sunshine and a cloudless, blue sky. The first 10 miles many horses greeted me along the way, running up to and then parallel to the road. For the first time I began to feel sorry for them, as they lived such a restricted life. My adventure had opened me up to challenges and experiences they would never know. Maybe their riders would one day make a Long Ride.

Howard tied me up to an irrigation pump in a little village, while he ate lunch. It was an uncomfortable stop for me, so I was glad when he returned.

After a 22-mile day, we rode into an RV Park in the village of Brogan. For only the third time this trip he paid to stay somewhere. The park offered some grass that we found, plus some residents gave me apples and a rancher delivered a bunch of grain.

Toward evening, Howard led me over to the café/bar. He sat at a picnic table with some local good ole boys for his dinner and conversation. One of the guys later delivered some hay to my picket line to keep me happy. Dave, Cal, Bill and Howard politicked for two hours before he led me back to the RV Park. I slept peacefully on the picket line.

We hit the road at sunrise after I ate breakfast. The sky remained cloudy all day and the temperature only reached 85 degrees.

All day long, I heard cries of many hawks but never saw any equine buddies. Howard tried to get me water around noon but the water tank was guarded by a single bull. Howard yelled and even threw a few rocks but the bull would not move. We gave up and luckily the next stock water tank featured heifers which Howard was able to walk through.

The only tree in the 23-mile day provided Howard with shade for lunch and more importantly, it was next to a lush alfalfa field for me. Howard took off the reins and I rewarded his trust by walking in the direction of Texas. After a hundred yards, he called to me but I ignored him. He finally got up and began following me. Being in a mischievous mood, I made Howard walk 300 yards to catch up with me.

"Misty, you little stinker!" Howard yelled. "What is the big idea? Were you walking back to Texas? It's 2000 miles away! Don't do it again."

He was upset so I never did it again. I think he was worried that I would not stop.

In the middle of the afternoon, we arrived at the tiny village of Ironside, which only had a post office and water. Luckily, Howard found an abandoned store with a yard full of grass. He poured out the last of the grain I had packed all day, so dinner was not too bad. He ate some food he had bought that morning. He strung my picket line between two trees and pitched his tent a few feet away.

After dark, he hooked me up and that is when the trouble started. A set of beady eyes caught my attention and I couldn't tell what it was. I pranced around and around in a circle trying to get away from it. Soon I tied the rein up in knots and I was nearly choking. I stamped my foot a couple of times, which woke up Howard.

"Misty, what's the problem girl?" Howard inquired.

I nickered and he bounded out of his tent with his miner's light on.

"Oh, girl. You are such a mess," he said as he unclipped the rein and straightened it out.

He stayed with me for a few minutes and then went back into his tent. A short time later, I spotted more eyes out in the field a short distance away, plus I heard the howls of coyotes. I got all twisted up again. That night Howard had to come out eight or nine times to untangle me. Neither of us got much rest that night. It was easily the worst camp site of the trip.

I was tired the next morning. Howard looked worse than usual, too. We stopped at a small ranch just west of town. An old cowboy poured grain in a bucket and dropped a flake of hay for me. Later, I saw Howard munching on something plus the rancher's wife poured cup after cup of coffee.

"Kale and his wife sure were nice, weren't they girl?" Howard asked as we rode off.

Indeed, they were wonderful and I kept trying to imagine what would happen to us, if there were no good people along our route.

Hard packed sand made for a perfect riding day. Ten miles west of Ironside, we stopped at a reservoir to quench my thirst. The shoreline was impossible for me to get to. Our luck held as an old couple poured a couple of gallons into my water bucket.

We reached the outskirts of Unity, where Howard trotted me onto a horse ranch. Howard yelled many times but no one was home.

"I don't like this Misty but you need grain," he said as he went into a shed. He emerged with my grain bag full. "I left a couple of dollars for the grain, Misty. That is fair."

Howard parked me on the north side of the café but there was no relief from the sun. After lunch, he led me across the street to the city hall where there was shade and lots of grass. After a short 18-mile day, the five hours of relaxing munch time lifted my spirits and filled my tummy. Toward dusk, Howard left me for his dinner. To my delight, he returned with hay. He looped the reins around a small tree making for a short tie. That night I saw no creatures or eyes, and slept soundly.

The next morning Howard must have politicked during breakfast at the café because we left late. However, the temperatures reflected the coming of fall. The first 12 miles were great with wonderful footing. Then the roadway began a steady climb into a national forest area. Worse, the shoulders featured new gravel and it was mushy, almost as bad as mud, doubling my work. However, I enjoyed having trees along the road for the first time since east of Salt Lake City.

We were loping along when a small pickup truck driver stopped to say "Hi." It was the horse owner from Brogan who had given me hay. His face was tired and weary and his voice was without life.

"What's wrong Dave?" Howard asked. "I am a volunteer firefighter and I am coming back from the funeral of the eight firemen who died last week. So many to die at once is overwhelming for me."

"As a police officer, I attended too many funerals of officers killed in the line of duty," Howard said. "I am very sorry for your loss."

As Dave drove away, Howard leaned over and said softly, "You never know about things in life Misty. Joy or grief can be found over the next hill or around the curve. Seize the day, because tomorrow is promised to no one."

Although he still had over a mile to go on his two miles of riding, Howard dismounted. He began talking as much to himself as to me.

"Misty, did I ever tell you why we are on this trip? Why I left my job to ride across America?" Howard said. "Two years ago, my brother-in-law Ken died suddenly from cancer. He had been a very healthy person all of his 49 years. He died six weeks after diagnosis. We were stunned and in shock. My own dad died at age 46. Life is uncertain for everyone. I had planned on making this trip when I was fully retired in 10 years. It's important to live your dreams when you can and not wait until you can't. So here we are 350 miles from the Pacific Ocean. I thought you should know."

A couple of miserable miles later we stopped at the café near Austin Junction for the night. Howard parked me at a tiny tree on the hill across from the café. The grass was short and brown but I ate a little. Howard had found grain near Unity and this

I ate with gusto. It was an uncomfortable night but I shrugged it off. I drifted off to sleep hoping tomorrow I would smell salt water.

The next morning started badly. Howard gave me some grain and began to walk towards the café. Halfway there he yelped and reached down for his ankle. 'Uh oh', I thought, that can't be good. Howard limped slowly across the street and into the café. If he can't walk, that means he will be on my back. After breakfast, he hobbled back to me. I could see him wincing in pain.

"Something is wrong with my ankle, girl," he said. "I took two aspirin but it feels like I twisted something."

He walked with a bad limp during the usual quarter mile of warm up. He mounted from the right side to avoid the pain of the injured ankle. As the left boot settled into the stirrup, a moan escaped from his lips. I broke into my usual lope as Howard gritted his teeth. Two miles later, he got off and limped the next mile. He seemed in less pain during the next session of riding me. After he got off, the limp had all but disappeared. Apparently, we had avoided a major injury.

We crested the pass. A panoramic view showcased the beauty of the next valley. A hawk pierced the silence with a scream as it circled in front of us. A green mantle of pines swept up the flanks of the mountains. A sparkling river glistened in the morning sun. The road we traveled was the only man-made aspect of the sheer, raw beauty before us. It was the kind of breathtaking view that Lewis and Clark witnessed in 1803.

The long downhill into the town of Prairie City passed quickly on good shoulders. Howard led me through town, stopping at an outdoor café for lunch. Two Harley riders let Howard eat at their table while I was tied to the railing. Howard enjoyed their camaraderie, since he was without human company most of the time. I too longed for the companionship of my equine friends. Both of us were feeling the deprivation from a normal life.

Outside the city of John Day, we stopped at a ranch where we were given a good chunk of hay. Entering the city, two little girls stopped us and asked Howard questions. After a few minutes, their mom presented a plate of spaghetti that Howard wolfed down. The trio then led us to the fairgrounds on the north side of town. A nasty cold wind blew up, as Howard put me in a small, fenced area.

"This is not good girl," Howard said. "It is supposed to either rain or snow hard tonight and I don't see where I can keep you from getting wet."

I had already turned my butt into the biting wind. I had no winter coat yet and if it rained, it could be dangerous. Howard scratched my muzzle and along the side of my nose for a bit--before he walked over to explore the site.

A Texas scream pierced the late afternoon stillness. I looked up to see Howard holding open a door to a building. Moments later I stepped inside and, oh my, what a wonderful sight it was! Someone had left about 20 temporary stalls up and several contained large amounts of hay. Howard locked me into one with lots of hay. He pitched his tent in the dirt. About 30 minutes later, rain fell. From the banging sound it made on the metal roof and sides, it was a fierce storm that dumped a lot of water. I was happy and relieved to be inside, dry and out of the wind. Though the temperature dropped to near freezing, I stayed comfortable.

"Rest day, girl," Howard announced the next morning.

'Yahoo', I thought. After 116 miles in five days, I needed to kick back for a day. After Howard returned from breakfast, he fed me carrots and grain he had picked up at the local feed store. Going outside, the first cool day of the fall was balanced with a sunny sky. Howard turned me loose on the thick, green grass that I grazed on all day. I noticed the hills around the city covered with snow. I had been so lucky last night.

We left the next morning in a slight drizzle. Howard had his rain gear on for the first time since Winter Park, Colorado. The shoulders were solid despite the rain and we made good time. Two hours into the day, the drizzle stopped and the day changed to sunny. West of town Howard stopped me in order to chat with two brothers who were riding their bicycles coast to coast.

Flat terrain dominated with a few hills. After a 32-mile effort, we loped into the small town of Dayville.

"Misty, I heard from the bicyclists that the local church will let me sleep inside," Howard said. "I just hope we can find something safe for you."

As we approached the small church on a hill, a woman came out to greet us.

"Where you from cowboy?" she inquired.

"Texas, ma'am," Howard responded. "I understand I can sleep on the floor of the church. Any ideas on where I can park Misty? I'll have to sleep outside with her, unless I can find some kind of paddock."

"She is welcome to stay in my back yard over there," she said pointing with her finger to a nearby house. "It has a fence which should hold her."

Howard broke into a big grin and I smiled inwardly at the thought of not being on a picket line. Howard found some hay to keep me from going hungry.

I saw Howard leave the church for dinner with the bicyclists who were also staying there. A couple of hours later they all returned, laughing and talking loudly.

The next morning Howard led me out of the back yard that was now full of my poop. Always the cowboy, he spent five minutes scooping it up with his gloved hands and tossing it into the field. Howard parked me at the mercantile store where he ate breakfast and bought supplies.

It was an easy seven miles moving downstream, finishing up through a narrow gorge. Turning left, the road turned steep uphill with narrow or no shoulders at all. The road widened out after a few miles as the sun rose high and hot in the eastern sky. A natural spring on the side of the road provided a welcome drink of water.

I spotted a steer outside the fence and near the road. The steer kept trying to go through the barbed wire to get to his herd mates. It was almost comical the way he bounced off the wire. Twenty minutes later Howard noticed a cowboy fixing fences and informed him of the loose bovine.

After hours of slow climbing, we reached a plateau. A rancher's yard yielded rich grass to chew on for 30 minutes, plus all the water I could drink. However, no one was home and Howard was unable to find any grain. The shoulders turned to either mushy gravel or disappeared entirely--forcing us to cross and re-cross the road many times.

Howard spied an abandoned, low-slung barn on the left side and that brought that 25-mile day to a close. The barn's corral offered a fair amount of grass in the one acre of ground. Moments after Howard entered the barn, his snoring trumpeted through the night air while I munched and later fell asleep on my feet.

We were out just after sunrise, even though the temperature was now cool in the morning. Force of habit I guessed. The shoulders continued to be lousy which had Howard walking me more than riding. A few minutes out, a stone stuck in my right front. It was quite painful and I refused to lope. After a few moments Howard asked me what was wrong--had I not slept enough and things like that? It took him a minute to notice the slight dipping of my neck with every trot.

"Sorry girl that it took me so long to figure it out," he said as he hopped off and began checking my hooves.

He removed the rock and we loped most of the way down the steep grade into the village of Mitchell.

Howard parked me under a small apple tree while he ate at the café. As I was munching on apples and grass, he crossed the street to a tiny feed store. Five minutes later his face was all smiles as he approached me with a full load of grain. As I ate, he announced that he had been able to buy a half bale of hay of which the café owner had agreed to place 20 miles further down the route we were taking.

I smiled inwardly and pleased that once again Howard had been able to keep me fed in the middle of nowhere. That evening the café owner brought out a guitar, while Howard and five bicyclists enjoyed an evening of conversation. We slept soundly in the tiny village park, as a cool, slight breeze kept the night comfortable.

We had our picture taken a couple of times as we left the village. The first eight miles were downhill before the road turned a hard left and up into yet another mountain pass. The shoulders were great and we made good time. Near the summit, a firefighter stopped and gave Howard two bottles of Gatorade.

An hour later, we stopped at a primitive rest area for lunch. While I rested and munched on the sparse, brown grass, Howard chatted with a state trooper who ran a radar gun.

"Where you camping tonight cowboy?" the trooper asked Howard.

"Probably in the woods just off the road about four miles further up the road," Howard replied.

"Any reason I shouldn't?"

The trooper explained he was a hunter and that cougars were no longer afraid of men. He said

I would be a tempting target for a cougar and that Howard should be extra careful sleeping tonight. 'Oh great', I thought. From alligators in Georgia, dogs everywhere and now lots of cougars in Oregon, sleeping continued as a risky business.

A bit further down the road, Howard located the hay and grain the café owner had dropped off. We made camp in a grove of tall pines next to a small mountain stream. A cold wind blew, though the trees blocked much of it. Howard looked me in the eye and scratched my cheeks as he talked to me about the cougars and how he would be extra vigilant that night. His face reflected his serious mood and tone.

"Misty, I sure hope nothing happens but I pledge to you that if you are attacked, I will defend you with my gun, knife and my life if necessary," Howard said.

He was dead serious. After he gave me a fierce hug, he placed his knife outside the tent, before crawling inside. I was short-tied to a fencepost. I peered out into the moonless night looking for threats. "Ow ow ow ough...." The howl of a coyote cut the cold, still night. I moved nervously around the post, causing Howard to wake up.

"You okay girl?" he asked. His voice calmed me down and I became still again.

Several more times the coyotes howled that evening. Later, the moon came up and I saw Howard's knife gleaming in the moonlight. Somehow, I knew Howard's knife and his gun were the keys to my safety. As the temperature dropped below freezing, the coyotes' voices fell silent. Howard on the other hand, tossed and turned all night and I believe he did not sleep well. I dozed off and on after midnight, wary of the presence of cougars.

The crack of dawn signaled a new day as Howard emerged from his warm sleeping bag and into the cold morning. His teeth chattered and he stunk like he had used both of my blankets to keep warm. He had a great deal of trouble breaking camp and saddling me because his fingers were stiff.

We were on the road at first light nonetheless and began the descent off the mountain. I belched steam out both nostrils as my hot breath kissed the cold air.

"You are a dragon Misty!" Howard exclaimed.

The moment broke the last remaining tension of the cougar-danger of the previous night.

A mile outside of Prineville the shoulder turned from sandy to hard-packed stones. I continued loping over them, even though it hurt me. I would pay the price for my stupidity the next day.

On the outskirts of town, Howard let me munch in a yard for 30 minutes before moving to the center of the city. We stopped and stripped my gear at a shopping center where 20 teens washed cars. Howard gave them five dollars to use some soap and water, thus I had my first shower in two weeks. He parked me on the grass near the Pizza Hut but I was not happy with the placement. Automatic sprinklers came on, soaking me. I protested until Howard came running out to check on me.

"Sorry girl," he apologized as he moved me to another spot of grass.

That new spot plus more carrots pacified me for the rest of Howard's lunch. He walked me south for a bit and we ended up at the fairgrounds and a huge field of grass. I grazed for two hours before he put me in a stall and threw his tent up in the adjoining one. I was tired from the lack of shuteye the night before. Feeling safe, I lay down and slept most of the night.

The next morning my hooves were sore. Howard walked me the mile to the west edge of town before mounting up. I only trotted a few yards before the pain forced me to stop. Howard hopped off and checked for stones and swollen joints. For five minutes he muttered to himself as he attempted to diagnose the lameness. Finally, he figured it out that the stones from yesterday had hurt me and he could not ride me this day.

"Misty, can you walk without my weight?" he asked.

Though my hooves were tender, I knew I could go at a walk without his 175 pounds.

Howard took off his spurs and put them in the horn bag. He walked around to my right side and I lost sight of him. WHAT THE?? I was startled as Howard shoved a tube far into my mouth and squirted that awful-tasting Bute in my throat.

"Sorry girl," Howard said. "I know the Bute tastes bad but it is good medicine for your pain."

With a look of resignation, he began leading me up the steep hill, as I tried to lose the bitter taste. Twelve miles and six hours later, we walked into a church field in the village of Powell Butte. After speaking briefly to the pastor, Howard hitched me up to a low fence, which was surrounded by lush, tall grass. Howard attacked me later with the tube of medicine, though I had to admit the pain had dropped off considerably.

The next morning my hooves felt fine as Howard swung into the saddle. I took off like a shot toward Redmond--covering the distance in an hour. We stopped at the west edge of town for Howard's breakfast. Since the grass was too short to eat, I was happy it was a short break. A few miles west of town, I noticed a sheriff's patrol truck turn around and pull in behind us. Howard glanced back to notice the same and stopped me. He hopped off as two uniformed deputies approached us.

"Morning deputies," Howard exclaimed loudly. "Was I speeding?"

The grim-faced deputies barely cracked a grin, as they asked for some identification. What followed was a series of questions about where we were coming from, going to, had we two horses at one point and had we ever been to a town not far from here. Howard was very polite, answering all their questions. They asked him to wait until another deputy arrived. Saying he was paid by the hour, he agreed to wait. Again, the deputies did not crack a smile. A handful of minutes later an even more grim-faced female deputy approached us and asked Howard the same questions. After two minutes, Howard finally asked what this was all about.

"About a month ago a man traveling across America left his pack horse tied to a pole near here," one deputy said. "The horse was near death and you and your horse fit the description of that man to a T."

A look of relief came over Howard's face when he heard the allegation.

"Deputy, as you can see my Misty here is in fine shape and I don't abuse her," Howard said. "Also, did the paint horse ridden by the other man have two eyes?"

"Well, yeah it did, why?"

Howard turned my head and the female deputy saw for the first time the hollow socket where my right eye should be.

She realized at that moment that Howard was not the horse abuser and it seemed all four of them calmed down. They chatted amiably for five minutes with Howard promising to contact the Long Riders Guild to see if they had any information on the abusive rider.

After they left Howard mounted up and we loped off. Howard chatted to me how he hoped to discover the identity of the rider who abused his packhorse. I could tell he was upset. We both knew there was no excuse or reason to have a starving horse. Too many people had helped us along the whole route of our trip. A few hours later Suzy showed up while I grazed on the side of the road. Moments later another horse owner showed up with treats, followed by Nickie from the local paper. An hour later, I was in a trailer for a short ride to Annie's place, where I would spend the next couple of days in my own paddock.

Howard said good-bye after he and Annie loaded me up with water, grain and hay.

"See you in three days girl," Howard said. "Enjoy your time off."

I had already viewed the snow-capped mountains to the west and knew instinctively that we had to cross them. Indeed, I would rest up for the challenge ahead. The yellow Volkswagen that Howard had entered slowly faded down the driveway. Annie came over with some tasty carrots and I savored the treat. After rolling in the dirt, I snoozed for a bit.

The days were wonderful with moderate temperatures and a whole acre of paddock to walk around in. Several large pine trees provided shade from the intense western sun. I ate non-stop grain, hay and carrots from Annie.

At sunrise three days later, I saw the VW bug coming back up the driveway. Howard popped out and came over to say hello, before he began unloading the saddle and gear.

"Almost done girl," he informed me.

I took off like a rifle shot, running hard toward the town of Sisters. At the two-mile mark Howard did not even try to stop me. The shoulders were great and OUCH! Something tore the pad on the rear of my right front hoof. I kept going as it was no big deal. Howard walked us into the town and tied me to a picnic table outside the café. He was about to go inside, when he whistled loudly.

"Oh Misty," Howard said. "What did you do to yourself? You have all kinds of blood spatters."

He lifted the hoof and spotted the tear.

"Not too bad girl," Howard said. "I'll be right back."

The wound had stopped bleeding and there was only a small amount of pain. Moments later Howard was back with a bunch of soap and hot water in a bucket. He doctored me for the next few minutes, ending by putting some medicine on the wound. Finally, he went inside for breakfast.

We walked past the rustic storefronts of the town, emerging ten minutes later on the west edge. In just a few short miles the landscape had changed from near desert to large, Ponderosa pines jutting a 100 feet in the air. Though the trees were too far back from the road to provide shade, they were still a welcome sign that a thousand miles of desert were behind us. Two hours later, Danika and a friend stopped by and brought out a horse 'picnic basket' with hay, water and treats. They had also brought food for Howard. We chowed down in the shade of the big trees.

Right after lunch, we began the slow climb up to the last major mountain passes of our trip. Right away, my nose caught the scent of burned trees. It became ever more pungent as I spied the blackened tree trunks and scorched earth.

We climbed for two hours where both sides of the highway suffered devastation by a recent forest fire. Even as a beautiful lake appeared on the left, it was surrounded by the black, ugliness of a fire-gutted landscape. Howard stopped to chat with a ranger for a few minutes before we pushed on to the summit.

The sun disappeared behind some clouds and rain threatened. A cold wind had replaced the warm air of Sisters. I would be cold if we remained on the summit.

"Misty, there is no place to camp within many miles of here," Howard said. "We are going to have to stay here all night. After I allow your back to dry off, I am going to put the blankets and saddle back on. That should keep you a lot warmer."

And so I passed the night with my saddle on, short-tied to a 20-foot tree near Howard's tent. The wind died down after dark and with the saddle on, I stayed warm.

Howard rose just after first light and by then, I was thirsty. I had not had a drop since noon the day before. Just to add to the excitement, my right rear shoe was starting to loosen up. Howard led me for several miles off the steep descent of the mountain pass. I sniffed the air for water and finally smelled it just after Howard mounted up to ride. I broke out of a lope at a mountain stream about 20 yards off the roadway. I saw there was no way for me to reach the stream but Howard could fetch some with the canvas bucket. When I stopped for the stream, Howard did look hard for a way to have me reach it, without success.

"Girl, I am really sorry but I just realized that I left the water bucket back with the couple near Sisters," Howard said. "I can't fetch you water out of this stream."

My spirits sank at those words and I was annoyed at Howard's mistake. I shook the thoughts from my mind and loped the next two miles of rolling terrain. After several sets of lope/walk, we started back up another mountain pass. Half way up Howard stopped for a candy bar and water. I knew he had to have water and food to do all the walking but it was still irritating.

"I am sorry about that water girl," Howard said. "I know you have smelled it in the stream for the past hour. The only good news is this effort up the mountain will be the last pass we will cross over on the trip."

Thirty minutes later, we topped the summit and looked out over a vast tree-filled valley below. Howard was gazing at this vista, when he began crying. He cried like a baby for a minute or so, reducing to deep sobs before quitting.

"I wish my dad were alive to know what we have done, Misty," Howard said. "He died when I was thirteen. I know he would be so proud of me and rejoice in our success."

In the four years I had known Howard, he had never mentioned his father. He never spoke of his dad again. It shows that every human has a secret hurt somewhere in his or her past. Behind every face is a story of joy, sorrow and pain.

The descent was gradual and Howard loped me a good bit. As usual, we dodged the reflector poles every hundred yards. As we passed one on my blind side, I felt the collision of the cantle bag and the pole. In an instant the leather strings snapped off and the bag struck the ground.

Howard reined me to a quick stop, yelling at me for being too close to the pole. I thought he was going to slap me, he was so angry. As he picked up the bag and examined it for damage, he calmed down as quickly as he had become angry.

"Oh, girl, I am sorry for yelling at you," Howard said. "You are doing the best you can and I didn't cue you well enough. We passed the pole on your blind side and you had no idea how close you were. I'm an idiot and hope you'll forgive me."

I stayed ground tied, while Howard found new strings and set the cantle bag back on. As he eased back into the saddle, he stroked my neck and told me what a great horse I was. The stress of the trip generated such outbursts and I forgave him. We were both giving one hundred percent everyday and that was a lot to ask. We both did the best that a man and equine could. An hour later I saw the first building since west of Sisters. Howard walked me over to a hydrant and drew water into a plastic bucket. I sucked down the four gallons in record time and waited eagerly for him to refill the bucket.

"Whoa girl," Howard said. "I will give you more in 30 minutes. I don't want you to colic."

Reluctantly, I was led across the street to some fresh grass. Howard stripped my gear and I chowed down. True to his word, he brought over another four gallons of water, which took care of my immediate thirst. He short-tied me with the reins to a small tree and went into the café for his lunch. We spent the rest of the afternoon on the grassy field with me eating.

Toward dusk I was munching away, when I heard the sound of a diesel motor dying near me. I looked up to see a woman leave the truck and Howard talking to her. 'YES', I thought as Howard filled my blue grain bag with what turned out to be equine senior feed. That day ended with a full stomach, not thirsty and a mild night. Nice to get lucky!

We left early the next day as the sun peeked over the mountain pass. It was a gorgeous fall day, not too hot or cold. The tree-lined highway featured solid shoulders and it was an easy morning. We had only been on the road for an hour, when the left rear shoe came off. Howard stuffed the frog area of my hoof with wadded up duck tape and then wrapped more tape around the hoof.

"That should hold you until we find a farrier, girl."

Around noon, a big Harley Davidson pulled over just in front of us. The rider removed the helmet to reveal a beautiful head of blond hair and judging from Howard's reaction, the rest of her was attractive, too.

"Hi Howard," the woman cried out. "Are you looking for this?"

She opened the saddlebag on the iron horse and out came my water bag.

"Sandi, you are a saint," Howard said. "You drove all the way from Sisters to deliver the bag! On behalf of Misty, I thank you so much for bringing it."

The two chatted as Howard slipped the bag over the horn and secured it. After 10 minutes the woman fired up the bike and drove back eastbound with a roar. I was glad to have the bag back. Howard explained that he had been a guest at the home of Sandi and her friend Mark near Sisters.

A few minutes after leaving Sandi, a car pulled over and Howard chatted with the two women. After they pulled out, Howard approached me with a grin on his face.

"We have a place to stay Misty," Howard said. "You will have a big back yard and I will sleep in a bed."

Two hours later we walked up to a house overlooking a river.

Howard and his new friends were chatting in the front yard, when the couple's large dog came up behind me. The 100-pound dog didn't bark or seem aggressive but I took no chances. I looked at him, pinned my ears back and shifted my weight a little forward. The dog ignored all of these warning signs and moved to sniff my left leg. In the blink of an eye, I cocked my left rear leg and struck the dog's chest with all the force I could muster. I noted with satisfaction, the dog flew through the air, landed in a heap and ran off. I had warned him!

The husband ran down the street after the dog as Howard apologized to the woman and hoped the dog would not need to see a vet. Howard stripped my gear, led me into the back yard, where hay awaited me in case the grass was not enough. I rolled for a minute before starting my munch time.

A few minutes later, a small truck pulled into the driveway and after 10 minutes, I had a new chunk of iron on my hoof. Howard asked me to be good in the back yard, before he slipped into the house to sleep. 'Not a problem', I wanted to say. It had been a tough three days going over the two passes and I was in no mood to be mischievous.

Howard did not emerge to leave the house near Cascadia, until well after the sun was in the eastern sky.

"Easy day girl," he announced, "just 18 miles."

The rolling downhill slope of the road combined with great shoulders did indeed make for an easy day. We stopped just inside the city limits of Sweet Home at some nice looking grass.

In the next 30 minutes, a couple stopped by to say "Hi" and left promising to bring back hay and grain. Before they left, a woman pulled into the lot and offered to let us stay at her house on the west side of town. She and the first couple exchanged information, so that the food would find me. More good luck for us!

Howard ate a big lunch at the Mexican restaurant--after he tied me to a tree at the edge of the parking lot. Several of the patrons came out to pet me and tell me how pretty I was. Howard took a long time to eat, probably savoring his first Mexican food in some time.

He walked me a mile before turning down some streets which led to the home of Bill & Susan. A fenced-in back yard backed up to a small, clear creek. I investigated my new home by looking for food under the stairwell, which led up to the wooden deck.

"Back, back, back," Howard ordered.

Reluctantly, I backed up four or five steps, until I was on the grass again.

"Stay out of there," Howard ordered again.

"Your horse understands verbal commands?" Bill asked with wonder in his voice.

"After 3,000 miles we are able to communicate quite well," Howard replied.

"Misty, over here," one of the couple's two young boys cried out.

I looked up to see a horse's ice cream sundae. Instead of ice cream with a cherry on top, it was alfalfa with sweet feed on top! The boys had also filled a bucket with water, completing my dinner. As the two lads stroked my sides, several photos were taken by their mom. Howard and the family disappeared into the house. Later that evening Howard came out to check on me and say good night. I passed a quiet night, munching and sleeping on the soft, green earth.

The day broke sunny and mild. Howard came out and gave me a ration of grain and hay, while he ate his breakfast. We said goodbye to the family and walked out of town. Perfect shoulders and flat ground made it an easy 15 miles to Lebanon.

Howard parked me on the grass along US 20 in front of the Big-Mart store. He stripped my gear and I flopped down to rest. Howard followed my lead and stretched his lanky frame over the grass leaving his pistol exposed. Despite my good rest the night before, sleep overcame me. My head plopped onto the grass and I was soon dreaming of being back in Texas. In my dream state, I heard Howard's soft snoring mingle with the sound of traffic. Suddenly, a sharp, male voice cut my slumber.

"Keep your hand away from the gun!" it commanded.

I opened my eye to see three police officers approaching us from the parking lot. Realizing they were officers and Howard likes them, I closed my eye and tried to sleep again.

"Is that horse dead?" the officer asked Howard.

No way was I going to sleep now, though I kept my eye closed.

"No," Howard replied sleepily.

"Are you sure? The horse looks dead. Let me see some ID," the officer ordered.

I suppose I could have opened my eye and stood up but this was too funny. I stayed 'dead'. I could tell from Howard's voice that he was still lying prone on the grass as he spoke to the officer.

"My ID is in my front right pocket, next to my gun," Howard said. "I am going to slowly pull it out."

After a couple of minutes, Howard stood up and asked how this all happened.

The officer explained that several people had called 911 that a cowboy had shot his horse and was now sleeping next to the dead horse. I laughed silently for several minutes. Howard promised to leave as soon as I woke up, plus to move over to a tree so passersby would not see his pistol. Laughing to myself, I drifted off to dreamland for another 30 minutes.

When I woke up, a man stopped by and offered us a place to spend the night. He returned with a trailer and I was able to sleep in a soft stall with lots of food and water. Howard came through again.

We were trailered back to the Big-Mart the next morning, where Howard quickly walked me over to a café. After breakfast he was walking me on the sidewalk through town, when my right rear shoe loosened. Howard surveyed the situation and put a bunch of duck tape around the hoof.

Near the edge of town we stopped at a saddle store. Howard tied me up and went inside. Ten minutes later, a woman drove up with a couple of nails. Howard borrowed the owners hammer.

"Misty, I have never done this before but I've seen it done a hundred times," Howard said. "I am going to try to use the old holes."

Howard's voice was filled with doubt about hammering a nail into my hoof. Eventually he was able to get two nails into my hoof and that was enough to keep the shoe on for the rest of another short day. At the edge of town, he hopped on and I was off like a shot. A couple of hours later we stopped at a roadside coffeehouse. Minutes later a woman named Wendy drove up with a truck and trailer. I happily hopped in, knowing I was done for the day.

We arrived at her small ranch north of Albany and Howard treated me to a long, cool shower. His strong fingers massaged all the muscles and it felt great feeling the sweat and dirt disappear. Meanwhile Wendy's husband Keith had filled a stall with all the goodies a horse needs to be happy. While giving me a shower, Howard related Wendy's thoughts on meeting him. As she and Howard were leaving the coffeehouse, Wendy realized she had picked up a stranger carrying a gun. Even though her friend Sandi had assured her that Howard was a good guy, she was still a bit frightened. After a few minutes, she calmed down and didn't throw us out.

"Mornin' Misty. How you feel?" Howard asked as he gave me breakfast.

I felt great, rested and was ready to ride to the coast that morning. Howard explained it would be a short day of riding because I had to have new shoes before heading out. A farrier came out and soon I had four new shoes to finish the ride. Wendy and Keith trailered us back to US 20, promising to pick us up after we had ridden through Albany.

An hour later Howard stopped and walked me over the Interstate I-5 bridge. It was the last Interstate bridge of the trip and Howard celebrated the crossing with a Texas "YeeHaa!" yell. Halfway through town a man bought Howard a milkshake. Passing a dozen kids washing cars for a special project, Howard stripped my saddle off. After paying the adult leader five dollars, he cooled me off with five minutes of refreshing water. He finished off the milkshake while I dripped dry. After we crossed a river on the west edge of the city, I was able to hop back into Wendy's trailer and spend the night in a stall back at her ranch. Lately we were only traveling about 15 miles a day, which was just fine with me.

The next day we rode from the river to Corvallis. The traffic was thick but the shoulders were perfect and the terrain was flat. Howard stopped at a market for lunch and was able to serve me up a pound of carrots. In Corvallis, Howard led me through the downtown and then a good mile to the Joan's apple orchard and my home for the night. Joan's orchard featured tall grass and Howard found some grain. Oregon proved an amazing state for hospitality.

Howard saddled me the next morning and walked me a mile to the café. He stuck me on the concrete outside. I was happy he ate and read the paper in half an hour. He walked me another mile before he was able to mount up. A couple of the miles to Philomath were not along US 20, rather beside a bicycle path. It was a nice change of pace. As Howard walked me through the small town, a man came up and offered to buy Howard lunch. Moments later, he tied me up to a tree outside a Mexican restaurant. The warm sun made me sleepy, so I flopped down and snoozed. Two minutes later Howard came out to check on me, muttering about how I had scared him. He had been eating his chips and salsa, when I had 'disappeared'. That made him run out to make sure I had not come loose and wandered out into the road. Silly Howard! I am smart enough not to run into the road.

There were a couple of nasty, narrow stretches west of Philomath, where the shoulder disappeared and the traffic whizzed by only two feet off my rump. The level terrain gave way to good-sized hills. Several cars stopped and the people wanted to say "Hi" to Howard and check me out.

Toward evening, Howard trotted me into a small ranch with horses just off the main road. He put me in a stall near the other horses and I promptly took a nap. Later he came out to give me more food and refill the water bucket.

"Sleep tight girl," Howard said. "Tomorrow will be a long and very different day for us." Different day? What had we not done in the past six months?

We started early on yet another mild, sunny day. We stopped at a café for Howard's breakfast. He tied me to the picnic table. Such is the life of a horse of a Long Rider—parked at a picnic table but given no food! After only a few miles along US 20, Howard turned me left onto a local road. After we crossed over a good-sized hill, the road turned to gravel! I had not been on a gravel road the whole trip. The lack of noise was wonderful and I dropped down to a trot from my usual lope.

We had traveled deep into the woods and had not gone too far, when a vehicle pulled in front of us and two men stepped out. They were a television reporter and a cameraman. We spent the next hour being filmed and Howard being interviewed. The hour-long break provided a welcome rest. After they left, Howard had me ride the next 20 miles with minimal breaks. The biggest rest came when we were stopped by a logging operation for 20 minutes.

Back along a paved road after the miles of gravel, we began to follow a small, slow-moving river. Sniff, sniff, sniff. The water began to smell funny. After another mile, my testing of the air revealed something I had only dreamed of for months--namely salt water. Salt water could only mean one thing. The end! I savored the words like a bucket of sweet feed.

A van pulled over in front of us and the driver stepped out to talk to Howard. After he drove off, Howard drew up close to me and looked me in the eye.

"Misty, I imagine you can smell the salt in the brackish water of this ocean estuary," he said. "Yes, sweetheart, we are only about 16 miles from the Pacific and the end of our long odyssey. We will be on our way back to Texas in two days. By the end of the week, you will be in Texas with your friends Leah and Scout."

Howard said with a soft, low voice, choked with emotion.

"Right now, we have been invited to a ranch near the next town of Toledo," Howard said.

As I launched into a lope, four horses in the field matched me stride for stride. It reminded me of an honor guard in a parade. Did they sense the need to honor my accomplishment?

My thoughts were jumbled as I tried to sort out my emotions. During the 180 days of the trip I had wanted the next day to be at the Pacific Ocean. Now that I was about to reach it, I realized that the adventure had energized me physically and mentally. I was conflicted about the end of the ride. What do I do after such a grand adventure? How will 'normal' life be again? How has it changed me? I guess I'll find out.

A few minutes later, the powerful, unpleasant smell of a wood pulp mill signaled the east end of Toledo. A police car arrived and we learned they would escort us through town. Howard walked me over a good-sized bridge, which brought us into the town proper. The chief of police stopped by and the patrol officer took a picture of the three of us. Howard led me through the business district and down the hill to the pharmacy.

The Knights had a trailer waiting for me to pop into for the short ride out to their ranch. After a 37-mile day, it was nice to be chauffeured!

Howard led me to a huge birthing stall where a feast of rich hay and grain awaited. Howard hugged me before saying goodbye for the night. As I drifted off to sleep, visions of Texas vistas filled my thoughts; the wind-swept plains, the boiling hot sun and the cool lakes near my home in Fort Worth.

The next day I was put out into the round pen beside the barn. I was happy and not surprised when I saw someone drive Howard's truck and my trailer into the ranch and park it. The man who stepped out could pass for Howard's twin but it was his brother the carrot man. I forgot his real name but not the carrots he always gave me when we had met in Colorado.

Toward sunset, a van pulled into the driveway and a couple stepped out and came toward me. To my wonderment, it was Joyce and her husband Lou. They had traveled 3,000 miles to see me!

"Misty, how are you girl?" Joyce said. "Ohhh. You look so fit and well cared for. We were afraid you would be skinny like we saw you in north Georgia. Howard finally started taking care of you didn't he girl?"

Indeed, Howard proved he was trainable, adaptable and since Georgia, he had managed to keep me in enough food to maintain my weight and strength.

On October the fourth, I was sleeping on the floor of the birthing stall, when Howard woke me long before daylight. I opened my eye to see him approach the stall door and open it. I brought my head around, signaling I was awake.

"Misty girl," he whispered. "Did you sleep okay? It is going to be a big day for us. I know you can smell the salt water. As I promised you in Salt Lake City, salt water means the end of our journey. Today we only have 14 miles of riding to the beach and then you and I will go home. Can you handle that, sweetheart?"

I nickered softly in response to his question and the stroking and rubbing he was giving my back and withers. Yes, I was ready to go home to Texas. Though I now enjoyed the adventure and challenge of the trip, I wanted to see my friends Lea and Scout, eat steady good food and not travel 23 miles every day. Howard moved off to one side of the stall and sat down. He told me we had 30 minutes before we had to get moving. We sat there in the darkness and silence of the barn, each lost in our own thoughts. I still had trouble believing it would end today. The road just goes on forever or so it seemed after six months. There was always another hill, another vista to see and then ride toward...no road? It did not seem possible. Knowing Howard, plus seeing my trailer yesterday convinced me that today was the last day. I dozed off. After 30 minutes, Howard woke me and slipped on my halter.

"You can eat breakfast in the trailer," he said, "while I have my eggs and coffee."

He led me down the path toward the waiting trailer. After I popped up inside, I found plenty of food. It was still dark this October morning as he fired up the truck. His brother Frosty joined him in the cab and we pulled out onto the gravel road.

Five minutes later, we stopped at a café. Not surprisingly, Howard found me a bucket of water to go with my feed, before he went inside to eat. Ever since the disaster in Georgia, he has been a wonderful friend and provider. From time to time, I glanced into the window to see him reading the paper or gesturing with his hands, as he chatted with his brother. As the pair exited the café, dawn broke over the town. Brother Frosty reached into his bag and pulled out some big carrots.

"Misty. Look what I have for you," he exclaimed.

As I munched down the carrots, Frosty promised me carrots every day, if I would leave Howard and take off with him.

"Carrots will buy neither her love nor her loyalty," Howard informed his brother.

He was so right. Anybody on the street can buy carrots but only Howard has made my comfort and safety more important than his own.

"But you are welcome to keep trying," Howard said as he tossed out the water.

We drove to the corner where we had been picked up two days earlier. I backed out of the trailer and onto the gravel parking lot. The morning rolled in foggy and a bit spooky. Howard did not bother to tie me to the trailer before tossing on my blanket and saddle. After he put the cantle bag on, I realized it only looked normal. The 12 pounds were missing. Thank you Howard. Reading my thoughts, Howard explained that the bag was full of crunched up newspapers and that is why it weighed less than two pounds. It was just for the photos to look right.

We walked off on the shoulder, quickly leaving the town behind. Off to our left was a bay that led to the ocean. It was filling up with small boats as the darkness faded. The putt-putt of their motors was the only sound. The fishermen waved to us.

The shoulders were firm and wide. Howard mounted up. I took off like a shot. It felt so good to run after a day of rest! Howard tried to stop me after two miles but I was too fired up to quit. I galloped on for another mile before he forced me to stop.

"Easy girl...we have three hours to reach the beach and don't need to run the whole distance," he explained.

With that he hopped off and walked his usual mile. The shoulder began to vary in quality so he had us crossing the road every couple of minutes. I ran much faster than usual because the thought of finishing made me a little crazy. We were galloping on the left side of the road, when 'Ughhh', a stabbing pain from Howard's left spur sent me onto the asphalt. A split second later, I looked down and understood why he did such an unusual thing. The shoulder had been washed

233

away by rain and there was a pie slice wedge missing that was about three feet wide and five feet deep. The gap was covered by one of those thick, growing vines. I had missed the difference but Howard had caught it and probably had saved my life and maybe his own. Whew! Even on the last day, we had to be careful.

The coast road was one short curve after another as the fog kept the sun from coming through. There were few cars on the road and we enjoyed the silence. After about two hours, we reached the resort and fishing village of Newport, Oregon. Howard dismounted and walked me over to where dozens of fishing boats were tied up. The parking lot was filled with their hanging nets and what Howard explained were lobster traps. A few minutes later, I heard the strangest animal sound coming from a pier. Howard was also curious and we detoured to investigate. Looking down I saw what appeared to be a huge blob of a creature with whiskers.

"Arrrf, arrrf, arrrf," cried the creature and I instinctively backed up in fear.

"Easy girl. It is only a sea lion. She won't hurt you," Howard explained.

Sea lion, mountain lion, I didn't care what kind of lion it was, get me out of there! When I started dancing in place, Howard quickly led me back to the sidewalk.

Lots of people snapped a picture as we climbed the hill out of the fishing village. We stopped several times to accommodate them. Entering a state park, Howard mounted up to take advantage of the soft footing and loped me for what would be the last time on the trip. After only 200 yards he had to dismount and walk me again on the sidewalk. There I saw the Pacific Ocean for the first time. It looked a lot like the Atlantic, except the waves were bigger.

"Only 10 minutes to the finish line girl," Howard said.

His voice sounded low and edgy as if he might cry. For the first time ever, his face was hard to read. I could not tell if he was happy, sad, angry or what. He simply held onto the reins as we passed by several motels and small homes. After we made a left turn, the ocean again came into view. Gray waves crashed on a white sandy beach. Mist rolled in from the Pacific Ocean. Seagulls soared across the sand and landed in groups along the water line. I saw gray sky past the mist that swirled above the waves.

Before us was a parking lot and I saw my trailer. This must be it. Howard began crying as we walked the 100 yards to the beach. Then he choked up and stopped. He cried a little more and then stopped again. I began looking at the beach to find a road to travel on. Surely this cannot be the end. Howard hung his head and looked at the asphalt, as my eye looked in vain for a place to continue the ride.

Where the parking lot stopped and the beach started, Howard mounted up. While a group of people took pictures, we walked the 150 yards to where the ocean met the sand. Howard urged me into the water but I still did not like waves and refused.

"Oh girl," he said. "Three thousand miles of travel through hell and beyond and you still won't go into the ocean. I love you!"

And with that, he hopped off and led me into the surf. A seagull cruised past us on its own journey. The little waves cascaded over one another and rippled over my hooves. I looked backward at 3,100 miles of America. I felt the energy of six months on an endless road across a vast continent. I took one look at Howard as he stared out into the surf. He looked at me and smiled. I looked back at my Long Rider cowboy and gave a soft nicker. As a Long Rider horse, it marked the end of my coast-to-coast journey across America.

EPILOGUE

Howard told me there are few 'last' frontiers on our crowded little planet--Alaska, the Matto Grosso Jungle of Brazil, the Congo, parts of Siberia, the Galapagos Islands, the Great Barrier Reef, the Outback of Australia, the Atacoma Desert of South America--and that vast, timeless, expanse across North America. I'm glad I carried Howard on this transcontinental journey. Many of my forbearers had carried men and women across its timeless prairies. My ancestors chased the buffalo, carried the mail, plowed the fields and pulled the wagons. Many suffered in various wars down through history. Some wild stallions still live in parts of the old West. But for me in my time, this was an unusual adventure with a good cowboy. He treated me well. Sure, danger existed on the road. Life or death? Yes, it could have gone either way. It was a matter of chance. He and I chose a Long Ride and all its dangers. The fact that I lived made the journey all the more incredible in the annals of horse history. For I am a Long Rider Horse.

ABOUT THE AUTHOR

Howard Wooldridge spent 18 years in law enforcement before retiring and moving to Fort Worth, Texas. He is a graduate of Michigan State University. He speaks four languages fluently plus horse. Howard has traveled extensively in North America and in 34 countries in Europe, Africa and Asia. He is a member of the Long Riders Guild, www.thelongridersguild.com and a fellow, Royal Geographic Society, www.rgs.org, London England. His next dream is to ride from Madrid, Spain to Stockholm, Sweden. Contact him at: www.howardwooldridge.org

Printed in the United States
38312LVS00001B/118-204